PROVIDING FOR ENERGY

PROVIDING FOR ENERGY

Report of
The Twentieth Century Fund Task Force
on United States Energy Policy

Background paper by
RICHARD B. MANCKE

McGraw-Hill Book Company

New York   St. Louis   San Francisco   Auckland   Bogotá
Düsseldorf   Johannesburg   London   Madrid   Mexico
Montreal   New Delhi   Panama   Paris   São Paulo
Singapore   Sydney   Tokyo   Toronto

Library of Congress Cataloging in Publication Data

Twentieth Century Fund. Task Force on United
    States Energy Policy.
    Providing for energy.

    Includes bibliographical references.
    1. Energy policy—United States.   2. Power
resources—United States.   I. Title.
HD9502.U52T93   1977   333.7   76-54731

ISBN 0-07-065617-7
ISBN 0-07-065618-5 pbk.

Contents

Foreword

Three years ago, in response to the energy crisis, the Trustees of the Twentieth Century Fund decided to sponsor a series of Task Forces dealing with energy. (Earlier, the Fund had provided support for studies of nuclear power and the need for a national energy policy.) The Trustees recognized that many other groups, public and private, would be at work on this subject and that the Fund's own efforts might be overtaken by events. Nevertheless, they decided to persevere, partly because they sensed that this complex problem did not lend itself to quick or easy solutions and partly because they were convinced that, by bringing together varied groups of authorities for intense and protracted deliberations, the Fund could make a contribution to the debate on energy policy. They realized that the Fund's effort might result in mere redundancy, but they were prepared to take that risk.

The first Task Force assembled by the Fund addressed the urgent need for financial measures to deal with higher energy prices; its recommendations, some of which have been acted upon, were a valuable guide to policymakers. Now the second Task Force has taken up the even more difficult task of devising a framework for national energy policy and procedures for its implementation.

In reviewing the record of the past three years, the Task Force found that energy policy was emphasizing parts of the problem at the expense of the whole and confusing the short-term situation with long-term prospects. The Task Force therefore developed a multifaceted approach for dealing with the crisis in all its dimensions. Thus, it distinguished between the short run, during which we must develop policies to minimize the necessary evils of dependence on supplies of foreign oil and natural gas that are neither secure nor cheap, and the longer-range task of shifting from dependence on these fuels to other sources of energy. Today, although no longer at the forefront of the public consciousness, the energy crisis is still with us. The Task Force therefore called for a much more concentrated effort on the part of both government and private industry, one that involves a reconsideration of our national priorities, to defuse the crisis and facilitate an orderly transition to a new era in which the nation's economy will have a wide variety of sources of energy at its disposal.

The Task Force held many heated discussions on many issues. Agreement on preferred courses of action proved difficult to arrive at because the problems are so difficult and the future so uncertain. But the Task Force persevered, managing to reconcile differences that at times appeared irreconcilable. In some cases, the participants decided, perhaps in an excess of modesty, that they did not know enough to speak with conviction. But they confronted the harsh necessity of less-than-elegant compromises and sacrifices of otherwise desirable national objectives. More than anything else, the report of the Task Force underlines the urgent and critical importance of prompt and effective action to keep the nation secure and prosperous in the long as well as the short run.

I want to express my appreciation to the Task Force for its dedicated work. Special thanks are due to the vigorous leadership of Herbert Cohn, vice-chairman of the board, American Electric Power Company, who conducted the meetings and focused the discussion with grace and energy. The Task Force was assisted in its deliberations by the expert testimony of Eric Zausner, former deputy administrator of the Federal Energy Administration, and Freemont Felix, a private consultant on energy issues. It also benefited from the presence of David Lilienthal and Benjamin V. Cohen, two Fund Trustees with both wisdom and experience in energy and related matters.

Richard B. Mancke, associate professor of international economic relations at The Fletcher School of Law and Diplomacy, Tufts University, wrote the background paper and served as the rapporteur for the Task Force. I am confident that the Trustees join me in expressing my gratitude to them all.

M. J. Rossant, **Director**
The Twentieth Century Fund
October 1976

Members of the Task Force

Philip H. Abelson
President,
Carnegie Institution
Washington, D.C.

Morris A. Adelman
Professor of Economics,
Massachusetts Institute of
    Technology
Cambridge, Massachusetts

Thomas D. Barrow
Director and Senior
    Vice-President,
Exxon Corporation
New York, New York

Herbert B. Cohn, Chairman
Vice-Chairman of the Board,
    American Electric Power
    Company
New York, New York

Michel T. Halbouty
Consulting Geologist,
    The Halbouty Center
Houston, Texas

Charles Hitch
President, Resources for the
    Future, Inc.
Washington, D.C.

Peter B. Kenen
Walker Professor of Economics
    and International Finance,
Princeton University
Princeton, New Jersey

Hans A. Klagsbrunn
Lawyer
Washington, D.C.

Walter J. Levy
President,
Walter Levy Consultants
    Corporation
New York, New York

John Love
Former Governor of Colorado,
Chairman, Ideal Basic
    Industries
Denver, Colorado

Richard B. Mancke, Rapporteur
Fletcher School of Law and
    Diplomacy,
Tufts University
Medford, Massachusetts

John R. Meyer
Professor of Economics,
Harvard University,

Report of the Task Force

PROVIDING FOR ENERGY

INTRODUCTION

Just over three years have passed since people here and abroad were shocked into an awareness of their dependence on insecure supplies of energy. In reality, the roots of the energy crisis go much further back, but it took the oil "embargo" imposed by a small group of Arab states and the subsequent quadrupling of oil prices by the Organization of Petroleum Exporting Countries (OPEC) to make the world community painfully aware of the insecurity, cost, and diminishing supplies of its most widely used fuel.

The first response to the oil crisis seemed constructive. Governments everywhere took steps to conserve energy supplies. As the world's largest consumer of energy, the United States was in the forefront of efforts to forestall the cataclysms then being predicted in many quarters. With great fanfare and the strong support of the American public, it launched Project Independence, which had as its primary objectives both increased conservation of present sources of energy, particularly oil, and rapid development of new energy sources. But then, with the lifting of the embargo and the disappearance of the long lines at gas stations, the official sense of urgency about the energy problem dissipated and so did the public concern about it.

This Task Force, assembled to assess the record of the past three years and to consider both current and future energy problems, has found that the initial American response to the crisis was inadequate. To be sure, some useful measures were adopted, but few have been effectively implemented. Both the executive and the legislative branches have put forward various plans for expanding energy production and encouraging its conservation, but much valuable time has been lost in efforts to reconcile their different approaches. Moreover, justifiable concern for the environment has presented formidable obstacles to the development of domestic substitutes for our present insecure supplies of foreign oil. Even the stockpiling of a strategic oil reserve, a relatively simple measure to counter the threat of another embargo, has proceeded at a snail's pace. At the same time, the United States has been accused, with considerable validity, of having done less than any other major industrial nation to conserve energy.

In short, the sense of urgency has been lost, action has been stalled by squabbling over piecemeal measures, time has been squandered. Instead of progress, there has been backsliding. The United States today is more dependent on foreign oil for its energy needs than it was prior to the embargo. Imports have risen from 23 percent of oil consumed annually (at a cost of $3 billion) in 1970 to a rate of 41 percent (at a cost of $35 billion) in 1976. The share of these imports originating in the OPEC countries has risen from 68 percent on the eve of the embargo to nearly 90 percent now, so that the nation is more than ever a potential hostage of a powerful cartel.

Accustomed to the blessing of abundant and cheap supplies of energy that have made possible our industrial might and growth, the American people have found it difficult to recognize and accept the profound change that has taken place since the dramatic events of 1973. That change, though, cannot be wished away. On the contrary, it must be dealt with in two dimensions. *This Task Force is convinced that the United States faces both a near-term energy problem that is just as critical as it was at the height of the oil embargo and a long-term energy problem that must be addressed now if we are to assure our future growth and security.*

In our view, the immediate problem is that, over the next 5 to 10 years, the United States will be forced to import substantial quantities of OPEC oil. As the embargo and its aftermath demonstrated, reliance on imported oil makes us vulnerable to interruptions or limitations on supply and to the imposition of burdensome price rises. We are not, of course, alone in our vulnerability. Few nations are in fact as well endowed as the United States in potential resources of energy. Most of our allies even now are far more dependent on outside sources of energy than we are.

Conceivably, OPEC or even a portion of its member states, in pursuit of their own economic or ideological objectives, may again take unilateral actions that endanger global economic and political stability. A disruption in the flow of international supplies of oil, bringing in its wake rising unemployment and declining industrial production and falling living standards, remains a clear and present danger in this nation and abroad. Even if the United States could survive a prolonged interruption in oil imports, the vulnerability of our allies would endanger our security. Under present conditions, our ability to shift domestic consumption quickly from foreign oil and gas to other fuels is extremely limited. So is the prospect for a substantial improvement in conservation of energy over the near term. Thus, it is unwise and unrealistic to suggest that the United States can attain anything approaching independence in energy supplies in the short run.

Nevertheless, the Task Force believes that it is essential that the nation take firm and forceful action to implement a comprehensive near-term energy program designed to assure greater availability of domestic supplies of oil and other sources of energy and to promote greater economy in its use. In our view, our present dependence on OPEC cannot be eliminated, but it can—and should—be lessened, thus reducing the competition for OPEC supplies and consequently the political and economic power of the cartel. While we cannot achieve independence, a lessening of our dependence can make a disruption of supplies or a more aggressive price policy on the part of OPEC much less likely.

Many groups, public and private, have studied the energy problem, usually focusing on either the near-term or the long-term aspect of the problem. This Task Force has learned much from these studies, although much still remains unknown. In calling on the United States government to forge an effective energy policy, we are conscious that we are repeating, in part at least, what others before us have recommended. But the nation has thus far failed to respond to these urgings. We cannot take much comfort in the fact that we have managed to avoid disaster so far. Even though the world economy has accommodated itself to much higher prices for oil, it has not found solutions to the near-term threat of oil stoppages or the vital, longer-term need to develop new sources of energy. There are no quick or easy answers to either objective. *But this Task Force is convinced that a dual approach—one that deals with the long-term challenge as well as the short-term threat—is essential.*

The world's conventional energy resources; mainly oil and natural gas, are adequate today and, for some countries, far into the future. The present problem does not stem from a true scarcity in the supply of oil and gas but from a potential artificial scarcity—or an artificial price—created by the OPEC cartel. If United States reliance on OPEC is to be lessened and the demand for OPEC oil proportionately reduced, we must expand domestic oil supplies substantially above present levels and substitute coal and nuclear power for oil in many uses; these changes in the pattern of energy production and use will require both time and huge investments.

Although expanding production of costly domestic supplies of oil is necessary to counter the near-term security problem, it cannot be relied upon to take care of our long-term energy needs. Oil is an exhaustible resource, and one day—no one can say with assurance precisely when—this now essential fuel will become scarce. There is considerable evidence to indicate that world production of crude oil and natural gas will begin declining a few decades hence, while the world's population nearly doubles. Alternative sources of energy are essential if the advanced industrial countries are to preserve even present standards of living and if poorer countries are to have any hope of sustained growth.

The transition to most alternative sources of energy involves an even greater time lag and larger investments than are required for the exploration and production of fresh supplies of oil. In addition to coal, nuclear power, and hydropower, we must also develop solar energy and other so-called exotic energy sources, for which the lead times are very long and the ultimate commercial feasibility is in many cases conjectural.

It is the view of the Task Force that the formation of a sound and effective energy policy for the nation depends on making a careful distinction between the immediate problem of lessening our dependence on imported oil and gas and the long-term problem of achieving a full diversification of energy sources. Such a distinction is not adequately reflected in United States energy policy.

Obviously, international developments, especially OPEC's quadrupling of oil prices in 1973–74, which had and will continue to have enormous economic consequences for the entire world, must be taken into consideration in the development of our energy policy. The already huge bill for oil imports at the current OPEC price poses serious balance-of-payments problems for many countries and liquidity problems on a global scale. We must expect further price increases, especially as the worldwide economic recovery increases the demand for oil. Such price hikes will pose some problems for the United States, but certain other industrialized countries and most developing countries simply do not have sufficient exports of other products to permit them to pay much more than they are now paying for oil imports.

The financial and diplomatic measures necessary to deal with these problems are outside the scope of this report. The financing of oil imports was the subject of an earlier Twentieth Century Fund publication, *Paying for Energy: Report of the Twentieth Century Fund Task Force on the International Oil Crisis.* But in the short run, the basic means of dealing with the threat to worldwide economic and political stability is the development of new productive capacity outside OPEC and stringent energy conservation.

Compared with many other countries, the United States has been especially fortunate in its supplies of energy. It has had ample domestic resources and, to a considerable extent, still possesses vast amounts, particularly when compared with such highly industrialized nations as Japan, France, West

Germany, or the Scandinavian countries. Although the total supply of domestic oil and gas is dwindling, the United States still has oil resources in great quantity and some short-term and medium-term prospects of discovering more. In addition, it has coal reserves that potentially are a greater source of energy than the enormous oil pools of Saudi Arabia. It also has uranium, though in limited amounts, and untapped hydropower resources that may be significant in some areas of the country. Because of its technological and industrial base, moreover, the United States has the capacity to adapt its consumption of energy to solar, geothermal, or other exotic sources as they become commercially feasible. So over time, we are in a position to make the transition to diversified sources of energy.

But the Task Force believes that it will not come about automatically. In historical perspective, this nation may have been spoiled by good fortune. Our energy riches have allowed us to become one of the highest per capita consumers of energy in the world. The American industrial machine was built on the ready availability of cheap energy, but cheapness also permitted and encouraged lavish use. From now on, the fact must be faced that energy will be harder to obtain and increasingly costly for American consumers.

A COMPREHENSIVE ENERGY PROGRAM

The Task Force sought first to reach broad agreement on principles and then went on to consider procedures. Thus, the Task Force determined that the first order of business is the protection of national security. Because OPEC or a group of its member states has the ability to undermine the economy of the United States and deter it from fulfilling its commitments to other nations through the threat or use of an embargo, the Task Force recommends that we build, as quickly as possible, a strategic stockpile of oil so that in any eventuality the nation will have time to apply emergency measures to keep the economy functioning. In addition, for the short and medium term, we must quickly expand production of domestic oil, whether offshore, in Alaska, or in oil fields that have been worked but not yet exhausted. Although there was some disagreement about the means, the Task Force was unanimous in its belief that we must reduce our dependence on oil imported from OPEC.

Paradoxically, it is the very size of the price increases imposed by OPEC that should make it possible to reverse the downward trend of United States oil production. At the old, preembargo international price, expanded production from United States oil reserves, where exploration and recovery are difficult, was too costly to be competitive. Since OPEC increased its price, expanded production and exploration not only for oil but also for competitive fuels, particularly coal, have become economically feasible in the United States. But the present system of domestic price controls works to neutralize this economic incentive, encourages continuation of high energy consumption, and, consequently, increases our dependence on imported oil from OPEC. *Thus, the Task Force believes that the United States must permit the prices of both oil and natural gas sold interstate to rise to a level that will both encourage conservation and stimulate increased production of oil, gas, and other fuels.*

The Task Force could not reach complete agreement on how best to achieve the necessary objective of raising domestic prices for energy. There was no disputing that the administratively easiest and theoretically most satisfactory approach would be the complete abandonment of price controls, an approach favored by some members of the Task Force. The resulting higher prices for oil and gas would create strong incentives to increase domestic production of these fuels, to conserve them, and to shift consumption to more abundant fuels, particularly coal. Our present reliance on imports of foreign oil would be reduced, and decontrol also would eliminate the need for the cumbersome and expensive Federal Energy Agency (FEA) and Federal Power Commission (FPC) programs to administer prices and ensure equitable allocation of domestic supplies of oil and gas, respectively.

But the simplicity of this approach was regarded as deceptive by others. Decontrolled prices would not be the product of the free play of supply and demand, they argued, for the international market for fuels is not truly free. The price of oil in the international market is now controlled by the OPEC cartel in the interests of its member states. As long as the United States remains a substantial oil importer, the domestic price of oil—in the absence of price controls or rationing—will be set by the delivered price of foreign oil. Price decontrol then would substitute the OPEC-administered price, which now or at some future date may be either too low to encourage United States domestic energy production or unnecessarily high and burdensome for the United States consumer, for the domestic price administered by the United States government.

In addition, decontrol of oil and gas prices is likely to create short-run windfall profits on existing reserves for domestic producers. The burdens of increased oil and gas prices could be more equitably distributed by the imposition of a tax on excess profits or a requirement that the companies plow back any windfalls into completely new exploration and development. If domestic prices are allowed to follow the international price, a future OPEC price increase is also likely to result in windfalls for domestic producers. This disadvantage of price decontrol could be countered by a temporary excise tax on domestic oil and gas prices equivalent to the OPEC price increase, a tax that would be phased out if United States exploration and development costs continue to rise. The revenues from the tax would be rebated to consumers through offsetting cuts in the personal income tax.

Another option, which avoids these problems of decontrol, provides for the replacement of the present price control structure by one that sets a price ceiling for domestic oil and gas based on the incentives necessary to encourage future domestic production. This incentive price—which would cover the costs of exploration, development, and production and would yield a return for investment and risk—could be adjusted upward over time to account for inflation and higher costs of increasingly difficult exploration. In the unlikely event that the OPEC price should fall below the domestic incentive price, import restraints would be imposed to protect domestic producers. The disadvantage of this option, of course, is that the administrative determination of price can at best only approximate the workings of a free competitive market and at worst—as the history of United States price controls for oil and gas amply demonstrates—will substitute political for economic calculations.

A majority of the Task Force recognizes the disadvantages of these options, but it believes that they, imperfect though they may be, are still preferable to the current counterproductive system of price controls.* Under present circumstances, the impact of the modest price increases on consumers and the economy as a whole is far outweighed by their salutary effect on energy production and consumption.

This Task Force emphasizes the importance of price increases in large part because they provide an incentive for greater conservation of insecure and nonrenewable energy resources. A few previous reports—most notably, the Ford Foundation's Energy Policy Project—have suggested that the United States could solve most of its energy problems if it introduced policies designed to reduce growth in energy demand below the 3.6 percent average annual rate of the 20 years prior to the 1973 embargo. But according to the Federal Energy Administration, even at 2.2 percent annually, the energy demand growth rate would be too high to eliminate the oil gap and too low to keep the economy from stagnating.

Mr. Hitch comments:
I do not fully agree with either of these views on decontrol of oil and natural gas prices. My own views are (1) decontrol should be gradual, for the reasons stated in the Report, but a firm commitment to decontrol should be made now; (2) standby controls should be retained to provide protection against possible future large and sudden increases in OPEC prices by permitting gradual adjustment to them within the United States; and (3) any taxes on windfall profits should be temporary. Reductions in income taxes, like all fiscal policy, should be designed to prevent unemployment and inflation, taking into consideration oil prices and all other relevant prices.

Although conservation alone cannot solve our energy problems, *this Task Force believes that an effective national energy policy must aim at reducing the average rate of energy-demand growth over the next 10 to 25 years without sacrificing the overall improvement in living standards to which Americans aspire.* Policies that encourage efficiency in the use of energy can serve both of these objectives. Government must encourage the private sector to replace existing capital assets that use energy relatively inefficiently with more efficient substitutes and must provide sufficient incentives to persuade consumers—both industrial and individual—that such substitutes are desirable and necessary. We are convinced that the price mechanism can provide just such an incentive for businesses and consumers to make investment decisions—on plants and equipment, processes, automobiles, housing, appliances—that promote efficient use of energy and large-scale conservation.

Over the long run, the Task Force believes that permitting the market price mechanism to operate as flexibly and as freely as possible is the best way to promote conservation of energy. But in some vitally important areas, additional incentives and disincentives—such as investment tax credits to stimulate investment in energy-saving capital equipment, excise taxes to discourage some forms of nonessential or excessive use, and mandatory standards to promote the use and production of energy-efficient equipment where the appropriate technology is available—may also be necessary.

We doubt that pricing by itself will be a sufficient stimulus to the massive investment required for the diversification of energy sources that the nation will eventually require as it makes the transition away from an economy based so heavily on oil. Private firms have already invested in research and development in breeder reactors, fusion, geothermal power, oil shale, synthetic gas made from coal, and the use of solar power in small-scale heating applications. But private investors lack the economic incentive to undertake the expenditures necessary to support a research and development program of sufficient scope to investigate the wide range of sometimes conjectural alternatives to conventional energy sources. *Be-*

cause developing new sources of energy is of importance to the nation and the world, the Task Force recommends that the United States government help finance such research and development.

This assistance, as we see it, can take various forms. Basically, though, the government should provide funding to the extent necessary to determine the potential of any new source of energy as a significant addition to our energy supplies. For those with sufficient promise, governmental assistance should continue until technological and economic feasibility are demonstrated and further development can be financed with private capital.

In subsidizing exploration of the feasibility of alternative energy technology, the government must avoid premature elimination of any promising possibilities at the early research stage and premature or over commitment to too many projects at the massively expensive later stages of development and demonstration. Assessment of the technical and economic feasibility of new processes is uncertain at best. The cheaper early stages of research and development provide a means for reducing the uncertainty and establishing informed choices for the selection and timing of commitments to the more expensive later stages. *Accordingly, the Task Force advises against the adoption of a narrow master plan for research and development.*

The creation of a comprehensive and effective energy program is a great challenge. It is made greater still by the need to attain a diversity of energy sources without unacceptable damage to the environment. Protection of the environment has recently been established as a basic federal policy. Although environmental legislation is often imprecise and ambiguous and has frequently involved costly or frustrating conflict with industry and individuals, it has achieved some genuine gains in environmental quality. *The Task Force believes that these improvements should be protected and strengthened where possible, not jeopardized, by the proposed comprehensive national energy program.*

Environmental objectives have sometimes been treated as if they were incompatible with energy objectives. The conflicts over the construction of the trans-Alaskan pipeline and the leasing of federally owned petroleum and coal lands are cases in point. Such conflicts are inevitable at times but are exacerbated unnecessarily when environmental legislation provides an open-ended invitation to litigation, which at a minimum means long and costly delays in developing much-needed projects to expand domestic energy supplies. Similarly, federal pollution standards have sometimes been set at levels that bear little relation to either the costs or the benefits associated with the required reduction in pollution. These standards frequently ignore the fact that the pollution problems facing different regions vary considerably. Moreover, industry is often fearful of spending what is needed to meet new standards because of the possibility that standards will be tightened in the near future.

While not attempting to recommend specific legislation in the environmental area, *the Task Force proposes that national energy policy embody principles that achieve a reasonable accommodation between the conflicting national priorities of environmental protection and energy-resource development. Thus, we urge that cost-effectiveness criteria should be given more weight in determining environmental standards, that cost-sensitive incentives and penalties should be employed to enforce them, that environmental standards once established should not be subject to constant revision, and that procedures for approving or disapproving projects should be streamlined.*

At the present time, responsibility for energy matters is diffused among a number of government agencies. No effective machinery is functioning to permit the executive and legislative branches of government—with the assistance of advisory bodies of experts—to cooperate in determining the objectives of national energy policy and developing measures to achieve them.

The Task Force is convinced the challenge posed by the energy crisis requires the same kind of response that motivated the nation in organizing economic recovery during the Great Depression and mobilization for war following Pearl Harbor. We believe that centralization of authority in the executive branch with the full backing of the President is essential, but executive leadership cannot succeed without cooperation of the Congress. Therefore, the

Congress should also reduce competing jurisdictions over energy policy. By doing so, it will not only strengthen the energy program but also provide effective oversight of it.

The difficult transition to alternate sources and efficient production of energy with a minimum of dislocation requires a national energy policy and government action to implement it. We present the following detailed recommendations in the belief that they will help the United States overcome the energy crisis.

RAPID BUILDUP OF OIL STOCKPILE

The United States should carry out as quickly as possible plans to create emergency reserves of crude oil and refined products equal to at least three months' supply of oil imports.

If the United States stockpiled emergency petroleum reserves, the costs of interruptions in oil imports would be reduced and the probability of any large oil exporter (or group of exporters) precipitating an embargo would be lessened.

Current legislation provides for storage of 60 million barrels in 1977 (enough to replace current levels of oil imports for about 10 days) and an additional 90 million barrels in 1978, at an initial outlay of about $2 billion. (This estimate covers both the costs of acquiring the oil to be stored—$11 to $13 per barrel—and the costs of constructing large-scale storage facilities, including associated ports and pipelines—about $1 to $1.30 per barrel.) The annual cost of financing this 150 million barrels of storage will range between $200 and $300 million.

The Task Force recommends that, once the initial 150-million-barrel phase is completed, a further, more rapid buildup of strategic oil reserves to provide, at a minimum, three months' imports (500 million–700 million barrels depending on actual import levels) be undertaken. This storage should be owned, financed, and managed by the federal government, which could raise revenues to pay for it through a small "security" excise tax on all refined oil products.

Some members of the Task Force, however, urged even stronger defensive measures, arguing that a three-month stockpile would not buy sufficient time to counteract OPEC political or economic pressure but would simply postpone unpleasant decisions. They recommend the buildup of a six-month stockpile supplemented by standby restrictions on consumption—a combination of rationing and excise taxes designed to reduce consumption by at least 10 percent, with special refund provisions for low-income consumers—which together with normal commercial storage could replace imports for about nine months.

Whatever the precise level of a strategic oil reserve, the Task Force urges that it represents the most effective short-term assurance against the imposition of an embargo or even the threat of one.

SHORT- AND MEDIUM-TERM SUPPLY OF OIL AND COAL

The United States must encourage expanded production of crude oil and natural gas from the Outer Continental Shelf and northern Alaska.

Large net additions to the rapidly shrinking reserves of crude oil and natural gas are essential to reduce United States reliance on oil imports. The delivery of oil and, subsequently, of natural gas from Prudhoe Bay in Alaska will only temporarily alleviate the secular trend to lower domestic production of oil and gas. The most promising sources for large net additions to the domestic supplies are expanded production from the Outer Continental Shelf (OCS) and northern Alaska. Development of OCS and Alaskan oil will lead directly to reduced reliance on oil imports and sharply higher revenues (for example, lease bonuses, royalties, severance taxes, and profits taxes) for both the federal government and the concerned oil-producing states. The Task Force also notes that, although oil spills from production in the Outer Continental Shelf are inevitable, reduced reliance on foreign oil imported by tanker will on balance reduce damage to the environment caused by oil spills.

The United States should also encourage a substantial increase in the domestic production and consumption of coal. Coal is now used primarily to generate electricity and to fuel certain large-scale, energy-intensive industrial processes. Because United States coal reserves are enormous and coal production can be expanded to meet projected near-, medium-, and long-term needs, substitution of coal for oil and natural gas in appropriate uses is desirable.

Coal production has been lagging, however, because of health, safety, and environmental concerns; because of continued uncertainty about price; and because of delays in the formulation and implementation of federal leasing policy. Yet the Task Force believes that, with a reasonable balancing of the different national objectives, the problems associated with the production and consumption of coal can be reasonably resolved.*

Most presently operating coal-burning plants have been able to satisfy federal air emission standards by using more low-sulphur coal and/or by installing pollution control equipment. Furthermore, enforcement of the Coal Mine Safety and Health Act of 1969 has led to substantial improvements in mine safety. Because strip-mining of coal is typically much less costly than deep mining, producers can afford extensive reclamation and, in many cases, under the requirements now in force in virtually all of the states in which there is any substantial strip-mining, are carrying out such reclamation. There are places in the United States where mining of any kind would damage irreplaceable recreational resources. But the need to preserve these sites does not justify resistance to mining in all areas.

*Mr. Hitch comments:
A possible exception is CO_2 from coal combustion, which some scientists believe may result in unacceptable climatic changes within a few decades.

SHORT- AND MEDIUM-TERM SUPPLY OF NUCLEAR POWER AND ELECTRICITY

Because of its large coal reserves, the United States will not need to rely primarily on nuclear energy to replace diminishing supplies of oil and natural gas. *Yet the Task Force supports construction of light-water reactors, which have the potential for generating large amounts of relatively low-cost electricity.* We regard such reactors as a necessary supplement to fossil fuel supplies.

A number of environmental and public safety issues are raised by the use of nuclear power. The most important of these are the problems of storing and disposing safely of radioactive nuclear wastes, the reliability of the light-water reactor's emergency core-cooling system, the danger in transporting spent fuel rods, and the security dangers posed by worldwide nuclear proliferation.

Extensive experience with light-water reactors in this country and abroad as well as a substantial number of both empirical and theoretical studies all suggest that the likelihood of a major reactor accident is small. Safe disposal of radioactive wastes clearly presents problems, but the Task Force believes that such wastes can be stored safely in the short run. We recognize, nonetheless, that a permanent solution to the disposal problem has not been found and that the more reactors we build, the more wastes will accumulate and the more imperative it will become to find a permanent solution in the long run.*

Research to find safe methods of waste disposal and safe means of transporting spent fuel rods will have to be continued even if no additional reactors are built if some of the dangers of

---

*Messrs. Abelson, O'Reilly, and Cohn wish to dissent from this finding.
Messrs. Abelson and O'Reilly conclude that a means of waste disposal has been found. Mr. Cohn believes an acceptable solution is clearly in sight; in addition, he does not think that the transportation of fuel rods presents a major additional problem.

nuclear power are to be eliminated. But the danger of nuclear proliferation will not be solved only by research.

Although 40 countries already have access to nuclear reactors, the United States, acting in concert with other supplying nations, should take effective steps to prevent the further transfer of reprocessing technology and promote stricter safeguards on the handling of plutonium and other fissile materials. We believe that serious consideration should be given to the proposal to place all nuclear fuel and reprocessing production facilities under multinational control, with the United States providing enriched uranium supplies to those countries that forego their own enrichment and reprocessing capability. There is, however, no necessary connection between the spread of nuclear technology to foreign countries and the expanded use of light-water reactors in this country.

To meet our own nuclear fuel needs as well as those of other countries, we must expand our uranium enrichment capacity. Present enrichment plants, making use of the energy-intensive gaseous diffusion process, are government-owned. The centrifuge process of enrichment, while never tested on a large scale, seems likely to use only one-tenth as much power. Current research on a laser enrichment process suggests that even greater cost savings may be possible. But in expanding our enrichment capacity, we must remain aware that cheaper enrichment will also facilitate the production of weapon-grade material.

Since domestic uranium reserves are limited, it may be necessary to supplement them with imports or with commercial processing of spent fuel. A decision to proceed with reprocessing, which produces plutonium usable for weapons as well as fuel, should be delayed until its need has been demonstrated beyond reasonable doubt. The same stricture applies to the commercial use of the breeder reactor, as opposed to its research and development.

The Task Force also believes that hydroelectric power, a renewable resource that, in some locations, creates minimum adverse environmental effects, should be developed and expanded where feasible.

OIL AND NATURAL GAS PRICES

The Task Force believes that the current price structure for domestic oil and natural gas must be revised to permit prices to rise to a level that will prompt producers to discover, develop, and produce new supplies of domestic energy so that the nation can reduce its imports to a safe level.

The histories and administration of price controls for oil and natural gas differ, but their effects on production and consumption—discouraging the former while subsidizing the latter—are similarly perverse given the present insecurity and future scarcity of these most widely used fuels. Since 1960, the Federal Power Commission has applied price ceilings to natural gas which have been permitted to rise at a rate much less rapid than that justified by the escalating demand. By 1970, the growth in natural gas production had come to a halt, and since 1972, natural gas production has been declining. Unsatisfied demand for natural gas has been diverted to crude oil, its closest substitute, thus contributing to our increasing dependence on imports from the OPEC countries. To avert serious gas shortages in those states relying on the interstate market and to encourage further exploration and development, the FPC recently allowed the price of new natural gas sold in the interstate market to rise to $1.42 per thousand cubic feet (mcf), although lawsuits to prevent these price increases are delaying their implementation.

The current price control structure for crude oil was established by Congress in the Energy Policy and Conservation Act of 1975. At the time of passage, the legislation rolled back the price of crude oil to $7.66—based on the average between price-controlled "old" oil and market-priced "new" oil—and provided for price increases up to 10 percent a year through mid-1979, when all prices would be decontrolled. By holding average prices well below the level necessary to encourage new domestic production, this pricing arrangement encourages consumption that can be met only by increased imports of foreign oil. To make matters worse, under the present system, refiners base the price of their products on the average cost to them of controlled domestic and imported oil, with the result that the true cost of increasing dependence on imported oil is concealed from the consumer, who consequently has less incentive to conserve on its use. Administrative difficulties in equitably allocating differentially priced crude oil among refiners and establishing fair prices for different grades of oil abound under the present system of controls. Yet most observers believe that the legislated commitment to complete decontrol of prices is an uncertain one.

The Task Force is agreed that the present inefficient, unworkable, and counterproductive system of price controls of oil and natural gas must be replaced. Two options for revising the oil price structure were considered, each of which was supported by a number of members of the Task Force. The first option provides for an immediate and firm commitment to decontrol of crude oil and natural gas prices. If all prices were decontrolled today, the price of domestically produced oil would approach the $13 delivered price of imported OPEC oil. Retail gasoline prices would rise 6 to 8 cents per gallon in the months immediately following decontrol.

Because the lifting of price controls may result in substantial windfall profits to the domestic energy producers, those members of the Task Force who advocated this option also proposed that it be accompanied by a provision that all windfalls be reinvested in increased exploration and development or that, alternatively, a tax be levied on excess profits. In the absence of price controls, the delivered price of OPEC oil will, of course, set the price for oil domestically produced. Consequently, to prevent additional windfalls for domestic producers, the members who favored price decontrol proposed that it be accompanied by authority to impose an excise tax on domestic sales of crude oil equivalent to any substantial future OPEC price increase. Because domestic fuel prices cannot exceed the delivered price of comparable-quality oil imports and remain competitive, the domestic producers would be forced to bear the burden of the excise tax, and the U.S. Treasury would collect the additional revenues produced by the OPEC price increase. Offsetting cuts in the personal income tax could be designed, although at some administrative cost, to relieve consumers of most of the financial impact of higher oil prices without significantly undercutting their value as an incentive to fuel conservation. With time, if the costs of domestic crude oil production continued to escalate, the excise tax would be phased out.

The virtue of price decontrol is the elimination of economic and administrative inefficiencies that are the inevitable by-product of any system of administered prices. But an attempt to take into account equity and other noneconomic considerations leads to the reintroduction of some administrative decisions, such as defining what constitutes windfalls and the excess in profits. Recognizing that political considerations cannot be avoided in the pricing of commodities as important as oil and gas, some members of the Task Force preferred the retention of the price control mechanism in order to refashion it toward establishment of price incentives for new exploration and development.

As a first step, this proposed option provides for separate pricing for old and new oil to eliminate the perverse incentives of averaging prices. Price ceilings for new oil—about $12 per barrel by the end of 1976 under the present legislation—would be allowed to rise gradually to take account of inflation and some approximation of increasing exploration costs. The old-oil price would be frozen at its present level of $5.50 per barrel, but the base volumes of production subject to this price would be reduced annually at a rate somewhat in excess of the average depletion rate in order to cover inflation and encourage production. Around 1980, all domestic production would be subject to a single incentive price.

At any given time, the United States incentive price may differ from the OPEC-administered international price. Under this second option, domestic price ceilings would remain in effect as long as the OPEC price exceeded the level necessary to encourage new domestic production. If the OPEC price were to fall below the domestic incentive price, domestic producers would be protected by the imposition of import restraints.

The members of the Task Force who advocate the retention of price controls point out that the controlled price of natural gas should be no lower than the equivalent price of oil. But they also point out that deregulation of natural gas prices in a period of acute shortages would drive the price higher than necessary to stimulate necessary exploration and would therefore result in large windfalls. Instead of the elimination of price controls, they endorse an amended regulatory policy explicitly directed at the establishment of an incentive price for the exploration and development of natural gas, which will come into reasonable parity with crude oil prices by the early 1980s.

MEASURES TO PROMOTE CONSERVATION

The Task Force endorses the use of special incentives to encourage further investment in energy-saving capital goods and consumer durables because conserving energy is as important as increasing the supply. Investment tax credits, excise taxes, and mandatory standards can help encourage such investments.

Higher prices for domestic oil and gas will help to conserve these fuels. Because the prices of other forms of energy will tend to rise with oil and gas prices, their conservation will also be encouraged.

Energy conservation also can be promoted through measures such as investment tax credits both for investing in energy-saving equipment and for converting plants and equipment from the use of oil and gas to coal or other forms of energy.

The Task Force believes that certain types of energy consumption are less useful and desirable than others and recommends the use of tax disincentives to discourage undesirable uses. Automobiles that consume large quantities of gasoline because of high-horsepower engines, air conditioning, and other devices, for example, offer an appropriate target for energy-conserving luxury taxes. Excise taxes levied annually and collected with state registration fees also might serve to encourage quicker scrapping of cars that consume above-average amounts of gasoline.

The Task Force favors the continuation of such energy-conserving measures as reasonable speed limits on highways, building standards that reduce the use of energy for heating and cooling, and requirements that appliances bear tags disclosing their energy-utilization efficiency.

RESEARCH AND DEVELOPMENT

The Task Force recommends an extensive program of government-supported research and development for new energy sources.

Alternative energy sources vary in potential usefulness and in what is known about their possible applications. Basic research of a high order is necessary to devise a production process for fusion that is even scientifically feasible. For fuels such as oil shale and synthetic gas made from coal, on the other hand, the basic technology for building a commercial-size demonstration plant is known, but high costs, concern for the environment, and uncertainty about future price regulations have delayed commercial development.

The program envisaged by the Task Force is not merely research and development but rather (1) basic and applied research, (2) the development of small prototypes to ascertain technical feasibility, and (3) the construction and operation of large-scale plants when necessary to demonstrate production feasibility and provide some indication of the costs of commercial production.

As we see it, the government should design its policy to supplement and encourage private research and development, especially on those alternative energy sources of which the least is know. Financing should be available not for the production of alternative fuels but for programs exploring the potential of new energy sources. The proposed Energy Independence Authority, which would spend $100 billion of public funds to subsidize the large-scale commercial production of several energy sources, should be evaluated carefully before adoption. The Task Force believes that, in granting subsidies, government should draw distinctions among the different levels of research, development, and design. Programs to develop the more exotic alternative energy sources, for which no basic production technology is available and the risk of failure is very high, need some form of direct government assistance.

National security, scientific and engineering capability, and the need for speed and efficiency in commercially developing new fuel sources are the most important factors to consider in deciding whether specific basic research projects should be conducted in government-owned and -managed laboratories subcontracted to private firms or supported by some type of direct subsidy to private firms.

Government subsidies of the later stages of the research and development process might take the form of loan or price guarantees. By reducing the cost of capital, however, such loans distort normal capital-market incentives and encourage firms to invest in technologies that are overly capital-intensive. The federal government could grant price guarantees to the firm that submits the minimum bid for supplying a specified quantity of energy produced by a process that the government wishes to promote. (A condition for this bid would be that the bidder satisfy certain minimum financial and product quality criteria as well as conform to legal, environmental, health, and safety standards.)

ENERGY AND ENVIRONMENTAL PROTECTION

The Task Force believes that concern for the environment, although important, should not be allowed to cripple the necessary development of energy resources or to promote wasteful uses of energy. The Task Force therefore recommends that, in setting standards, drafting laws, or devising administrative procedures to protect the environment,

*policymakers seek to reconcile the goals of environmental protection
with those of energy policy.*

Environmental protection is clearly a vital policy objective.
The apparent conflicts between this objective and that of
energy policy can be resolved according to a very few basic
principles:

- Standards for the prevention or alleviation of pollution
  or environmental damage must be clear and enforce-
  able. Uncertainty about shifting standards must be
  eliminated so that industry will be able to plan ahead.

- Speed is essential to the effective implementation of
  policy decisions in these areas. The increasing availability of research findings on environmental and energy
  issues should expedite administrative decision making.

- Conflicts in authority must be eliminated, and the administrative procedures for testing, judgment, and ap-
  peal must be made known to all interested parties.

- Cost-effectiveness criteria must be given more weight
  in the application of environmental standards. In many
  cases, the environmental standards now in effect provide only marginal benefits at costs great enough to
  impede production and the development of new resources. We believe that policymakers should weigh
  benefits to the environment against costs to the
  economy or to energy-resource development in establishing environmental standards. When incentives and
  penalties are imposed to enforce standards, they
  should also be sensitive to costs.

- In setting environmental standards, policymakers
  should treat pollution resulting from productive activities that serve essential policy purposes more le-
  niently than pollution resulting from a nonessential use
  or process. They should compensate for greater leeway
  allowed to energy producers or conservers by imposing
  stricter standards, strictly enforced, on some non-
  energy sectors.

- National standards must be flexible enough to accommodate regional differences. Uniform national standards greatly increase costs.

GOVERNMENTAL ORGANIZATIONS

To create a governmental structure adequate to the enormous task of developing and managing an effective long-range energy program for the United States, the Task Force recommends that a national administrator be given authority to coordinate the major energy functions now dispersed throughout the government and that a joint committee on energy be established in Congress.

United States energy policymaking continues to be plagued by indecision, uncertainty, contradiction, and delay that can be properly dealt with only if the Congress and the President first specify the appropriate goals for a national energy policy and then appoint an administrator with the power to coordinate, develop, and implement that policy.

We believe that a national energy administrator, with ready access to the President, should have authority over the national energy program. This official should work with representatives of the Cabinet departments involved with energy policy. We recommend that the national energy administrator coordinate the major functions and activities relating to development of energy that are now dispersed throughout the government. Where such coordination might cause delays, the administrator should have the power to issue directives in the name of the President, specifying the action to be taken.

An advisory committee consisting of both government agencies that have a stake in energy and private individuals should be set up to work with the national energy administrator and to promote public understanding of the issues.

Congress should organize a joint committee on energy, patterned after the Joint Committee on Atomic Energy, to deal with the legislative aspects of the energy program. If a particular committee's power cannot or should not be transferred to the joint committee, combined hearings should regularly be held by that committee and the joint committee to avoid unnecessary duplication.

In 1973–74, the public was awakened to the threat of a nationwide energy shortage and responded in a patriotic manner to appeals to modify its energy consumption. This enthusiasm and willingness to sacrifice slowly evaporated because of a failure of government leadership. The momentum that could have sustained radical shifts in energy policy was dissipated, but the lifting of the embargo did not change the fact that a new era had begun.

The United States no longer possesses the wealth of energy resources that once provided cheap fuel for its industrial growth and permitted Americans to consume energy as if the supply were inexhaustible, but it still possesses technological and entrepreneurial skills and traditional American ingenuity. These qualities can and should make the declining availability of oil and gas an opportunity, not a misfortune. What is needed to make the American people recognize and respond to this challenge is vigorous leadership in pursuit of clear objectives.

The Task Force has set forth the practical goals of a national energy policy and has outlined a series of specific measures for their attainment in the third century since the founding of the United States. If the nation's leadership provides adequate direction, the Task Force believes that the American people will respond.

ADDITIONAL VIEWS OF HERBERT B. COHN

It is inevitable that the report of a Task Force will vary from what any individual member of the Task Force would regard as the optimum in content and emphasis. I join in the major conclusions and recommendations in the report. I feel compelled, however, to add a few additional comments and, in some respects, to suggest some differences in emphasis. More specifically:

1. An essential point that is perhaps implicit in the report, but which I believe merits the greatest emphasis, is to underscore the high degree of correlation between an adequate and reliable energy supply and our economy, employment, and standard of living. Abundant energy has been essential to the economic development of the United States. It is even more essential now. Without it, our nation cannot sustain the high standard of living that most of our citizens enjoy. More important, an inadequacy of energy supply will impose a major obstacle to improvements in the standard of living of our economically disadvantaged. This latter point has been made in forceful terms by Bayard Rustin in an article in the *New York Times* of May 2, 1976. Similarly, the well-being of the industrialized world and the possibilities for an improved standard of living in the developing countries are dependent on access to secure and adequate energy supplies. All of this further emphasizes the need for a sense of real urgency in the development and implementation of a sound energy policy.

2. As a practical matter, coal, uranium, water power, and most of the more exotic new sources of energy are usable, for the most part, only by conversion into electricity. Electric power now represents about 27 percent of our total energy consumption. There is general aggrement on the need to provide substitutes for oil and gas wherever such substitution is feasible. Such substitution, and utilization of new sources of energy, will

be primarily through the use of electricity. The consensus of opinion is that electric power will provide some 50 percent of total energy by the year 2000. Our energy policy must therefore assure that the necessary capital can be attracted to finance the required electric power facilities and that the necessary authorization can be obtained to build such facilities without interminable delays. This is essential in the short and medium term to utilize our domestic resources of coal, uranium, and hydropower and in the long term to use the newly developed sources of energy.

3. There has been a great deal of obfuscation in the national debate on whether we can have both an adequate supply of energy and maintenance and enhancement of the environment. The fact is that we cannot have pristine air and water on the one hand and an industrialized economy and a high standard of living on the other. There are some inevitable conflicts, and there must necessarily be an accommodation and trade-offs to achieve a compromise that best furthers the overall public interest.

Where the emphasis on environmental enhancement is in eliminating even minimal and highly speculative hazards to health without any regard for the obstacles that may be imposed in the way of energy development, it is relevant and, in the context of the circumstances we face today, probably actuarially sound to point out (as it was recently in Denver's *Rocky Mountain News*) that "it is far more likely that our children will die in a war for energy than from the pollution that energy causes."[1] And where the concept of environment is somewhat broader and is related to the quality of life, it is equally pertinent to refer to the observation made by Edward Teller that a major aspect of the environmental problem is "pollution by poverty" and that "no environment problem is more important, or is harder to relieve, than world-wide poverty. Energy is one of the keys to solving the problem."[2]

The need to achieve a proper balance between these competing and sometimes conflicting interests cannot be accomplished where those charged with responsibility for environmental enhancement have the power to veto or delay interminably proposed actions to achieve energy development. Ultimately, there must be someone with authority to balance all relevant considerations and to authorize action that reflects accommodation of all aspects of the public interest. This is lacking in our present governmental organization and, at least in my view, must be an essential part of a sound energy policy.

4. The report advocates excise taxes to discourage "nonessential," "excessive," or "undesirable" uses of energy. I join in the recommendation for the removal of artificial ceilings on prices for domestic oil and gas so that the price charged will represent a more accurate signal as to their true cost and will help to conserve such fuels for higher uses. At the same time, I have considerable reservations about imposing excise taxes where the primary objective is not to produce revenue but instead to discourage use by artifically increasing prices. I question the validity of such an approach for at least two principal reasons. First, as a practical matter, the principal effect of artifically increased prices is to discourage use by the less economically advantaged; those in the high economic brackets are less influenced by price and will therefore be much less influenced to curtail their use. Second, and perhaps even more important, I have a distrust of the subjective value judgments required to decide what are nonessential, excessive, or undesirable uses. We have already seen the dangers inherent in the mechanisms now available to enable one group to impose its subjective life-style judgments on another. To some extent, this may be inescapable. But in my view, we should be very hesitant to extend this approach beyond the essential minimum.

NOTES

[1]"Nuclear Development," *Electrical World,* August 15, 1976, quoting H. Peter Metzger in the *Rocky Mountain News.*
[2]Edward Teller, "My Turn: Nuclear Salvation," *Newsweek,* May 17, 1976.

ADDITIONAL COMMENTS OF M. A. ADELMAN, PETER B. KENEN, AND JOHN R. MEYER

Although we agree with most of the recommendations of the Report, we must add some major qualifications.

A basic misconception throughout the report is that we are involved in an energy "shortage" or gap, to be filled partly by conserving energy and partly by expanding production. In fact, no such gap exists or can exist (except momentarily or when governments hold the price down below the competitive level). The OPEC monopoly will keep raising the world price either directly or by restricting output. They will do this as they have since 1970, in installments. But either way, there will be plenty of oil for anyone able to pay. No monopolist wants his customers to do without—it costs him money. The case for conservation and expanded production is, therefore, the case for reducing the price we will have to pay—not for closing any preordained gap.

We have two real problems: the security of the oil supply and the price of energy.

I

On security, the Task Force analysis is factually and logically inadequate. The frequent references to the Arab oil "embargo" of 1973–74 perpetuate a myth. There was, and can be, no selective Arab embargo against the United States. United States imports are, and long will be, well below the capacity of the non-Arab producers, who gain both politically and financially by diverting supply from other customers to the United States. Accordingly, the "hostile" United States, as the Arabs saw us, suffered no more import reduction than the "friendly" French or British or the "odiously neutral" Japanese.

What really happened was a substantial production cut, which quadrupled the price and caused great fear of physical dearth. Since friendly nations import much more of their oil than does the United States, they suffered more than we did. The same thing will happen next time. Even if the United States cuts imports to zero, our friends will remain vulnerable, and we will be vulnerable in consequence. Neither increased production nor reduced consumption in this country can relieve us from political or economic blackmail. Hence "energy independence" is simply impossible. It is not true that "expanding production of costly domestic supplies of oil is necessary to counter the near-term security problem" (p. 6). The problem is the loss of a large part of supply for a limited period. The permanent assurance of a very small increment, not available for years to come, is a truly "costly" irrelevance.

A larger stockpile than recommended by the majority of the Task Force, built up more rapidly, will give us some grounds for urging similar faster action on other consuming nations. At present, we are engaged in useless and undignified argument with them over "conservation," which promises nothing for security or for lower prices.

II

Security aside, public policy should aim only to reduce the costs of energy to the American economy, not to cover any shortage. A barrel newly saved is like a barrel newly produced. If the capital or labor or just personal inconvenience needed to save or create the barrel costs less than the OPEC price, the nation has saved resources. But to produce domestic energy, or to conserve it, at a cost above the OPEC price is a deadweight economic loss. Far from our seeking such conservation or new production, we should do all we can to avoid it.

What public policy can do is to create new options for *lower-cost* energy. We therefore welcome the report's emphasis on research and development and also its opposition to "the adoption of a narrow master plan for research and development" (p. 13). The equivocal reference to the Energy Independence Authority (p. 25) contradicts the previous sentence and should be stricken. The proposed $100 billion waste should be rejected.

III

The outstanding shortcoming of the Task Force report is its failure to recommend forthrightly the prompt, complete decontrol of oil and gas prices.

By holding these prices down, we create shortages because we encourage consumers to demand additional imported oil, natural gas, and synthetic gas and oil—in order of rising costs. The mischief is compounded by rolling in or averaging these high prices with the subsidized lower ones. Consumers literally do not know what is happening to them and take no action to substitute less expensive energy-using equipment. Thus, we ultimately raise energy costs to consumers and the national economy.

An "incentive price" is illusory—nobody can estimate it with the requisite precision.

Decontrol need not be immediate since the desired effect is on investment behavior. Producers need time to find new deposits and build new facilities; consumers need time to switch to less energy-intensive methods and to less scarce fuels. To move immediately to higher price in 1976 would not add much to the effect of assuring an uncontrolled price by 1979; the incentive to invest *now* is the firm assurance of a higher price by 1979, when investment now will start to give us more production or less consumption. But there should be an immediate commitment to decontrol.

The report, at page 10, confuses two utterly different market structures. The world monopoly sets a price that is an external fact to domestic energy producers, who are competitive price takers.

High oil prices are a burden we deplore. But the high world price is a fact, and it is an expensive harmful act to ignore it. A ceiling on domestic prices favors those refiners who can obtain the cheaper domestic crude oil. To equalize competition, we are forced to award compensating payments ("entitlements") to importers, who pay higher world prices. The net result is that we are paying bounties to those who import oil while levying a penalty on those who produce it at home. We commit a similar folly by holding natural gas prices down to a small fraction of current oil equivalent, thereby encouraging imports of gas at prices much higher than oil. A coherent energy price structure, accepting the world price level as a fact, will cost consumers less than price controls.

Background Paper

By Richard B. Mancke

1

Introduction

In October 1973, the renewal of warfare between Israel and its Arab foes prompted members of the Organization of Arab Petroleum Exporting Countries (OAPEC) to cut back their oil exports an estimated 4.5 million barrels per day.[1] Most oil-importing countries, unable to find adequate substitutes for Arab oil at short notice, suffered oil shortages. By late December 1973, the price of a barrel of crude oil at the Persian Gulf had tripled, rising to about $8, and small quantities of crude were being sold in the spot market for as much as $20 per barrel.[2] Higher oil prices and supply shortages caused all oil consumers to suffer real deprivation.

The OAPEC embargo marked the first time since the War of 1812 that the United States had been a victim of prolonged economic warfare. It also damaged vital national security interests. The cohesion of the Western alliance was weakened considerably by the industrialized countries' inability to cope with sudden fuel shortages and soaring energy prices. And OAPEC's success in using the embargo tactic to promote its economic and political aims created a precedent that that group and others might well follow in future international conflicts.

The United States needs massive quantities of energy to fuel its economy. In 1976, Americans are expected to consume 74 quadrillion British thermal units (Btu) of energy at a cost of about $150 billion.[3] Three fossil fuels—crude oil, natural gas, and coal—account for more than 90 percent of the total primary energy consumed in the United States[4] (see Table 1). Nuclear power accounts for only about 2 percent, but its share is projected to grow rapidly in the near future. The United States produces virtually all of the coal and nuclear and more than 90 percent of the natural gas it needs. But it must import 42 percent of the 6.3 billion barrels of crude oil and refined product equivalents projected to be consumed in 1976. Even if the United States adopts policies to promote energy conservation and accelerate production of domestic energy supplies, substantial reliance on oil imports is inevitable for at least the next 15 years.

Events following the embargo demonstrate that substantial reliance on potentially insecure oil imports poses two dangers to the United States economy. The first danger arises because it is impossible for any nation to reduce its energy consumption immediately and substantially without suffering

Table 1 Forecast of U.S. Primary Energy Demand

PRODUCT	1974 (PRELIMINARY)	1975 (FORECAST)	1976 (FORECAST)*
		(QUADRILLION BTU)	
Crude oil (including natural gas liquids)	33.49	33.16	34.7
	(45.8%)	(46.1%)	(46.8%)
Natural gas	22.24	20.65	20.03
	(30.4%)	(28.7%)	(27.0%)
Coal	13.17	13.36	14.03
	(18.0%)	(18.6%)	(18.9%)
Nuclear	1.17	1.80	2.43
	(1.6%)	(2.5%)	(3.3%)
Hydro, etc.	3.05	3.00	3.00
	(4.2%)	(4.2%)	(4.0%)
Total	73.12	71.96	74.18

*The 1976 forecast is premised on the assumption that real GNP grows by 5 percent.

Source: Address by John Lichtblau, executive director of the Petroleum Industry Research Foundation, reprinted in "Pirnic Sees Rising Energy, Oil Demand," *Oil and Gas Journal,* November 24, 1975, p. 30.

real deprivation. A great deal of energy is consumed in all sectors of the American economy: residential, commercial, industrial, and transportation (see table 2). Most of this energy either fuels long-lived capital assets and consumer durables or provides process and space heat. Given both the nation's existing stock of factories, machinery, appliances, residential and commercial structures, and transportation media and the fact that producers of domestic fuels have very little spare capacity, any sudden, sustained interruption in the flow of oil imports necessitates offsetting cutbacks in fuel consumption. Because it will take several years to introduce more energy-efficient substitutes for many of these capital assets and consumer durables, a sizable interruption of oil imports would impair the economic well-being of the United States in two ways: it would force many energy-intensive businesses to institute corresponding production cutbacks almost immediately, and it would require most consumers to reduce their consumption of gasoline and heating oils by roughly proportionate amounts. Sudden production cutbacks by business would result in higher unemployment, lower GNP, and lower living standards. Likewise, reduced gasoline and fuel oil supplies would force consumers to reduce home and office temperatures to levels many judge uncomfortable and would curtail not only pleasure but also business-related driving.

Substantial reliance on oil imports poses a second danger to the United States economy because domestic production of the major kinds of energy cannot be expanded appreciably in

Table 2   1973 U.S. Energy Consumption by Major Sectors

SECTOR	TOTAL CONSUMPTION (QUADRILLION BTU)
Residential	16.3
Commercial	10.4
Industrial	29.5
Transportation	18.8

Source: Energy Policy Project of the Ford Foundation, *A Time to Choose* (Cambridge, Mass.: Ballinger, 1974), p. 21.

the near future. Sharp rises in the price of oil imports create strong pressures for corresponding price hikes in domestically produced fuels. But spending on energy already accounts for roughly 10 percent of the United States' total GNP. Thus, sharp increases in energy prices would indirectly reduce American consumers' purchasing power and ultimately reduce their economic well-being.[5]

The economic and security problems resulting from the oil embargo and the soaring price of oil imports have forced United States policymakers to focus their attention on energy matters. Nonetheless, national interest in energy issues is not of recent vintage. For at least the last 75 years, four basic objectives have vied for priority in the formulation of energy policy.

One goal has been to acquire, as efficiently as possible, sufficient energy supplies to fuel the economy. Another goal, especially during World War II, has been to ensure that the flow of these supplies was not interrupted by hostile foreign nations. A third goal has been to distribute energy-related costs and benefits more equitably among producers and consumers. A fourth goal has been to reduce the environmental damage and public health and safety risks posed by the production, transportation, and consumption of various fuels.

Because the nation's energy goals frequently conflict, it is important for policymakers to address these questions: Which public sectors should assign priorities among energy goals? How can policymakers resolve the discrepancies in public evaluations of the priority each goal should receive? Which policies have contributed to these perceived conflicts? And how can policies be reformulated to achieve these goals with minimum conflict or disruption to society?

2

The Problems of Increasing
Domestic Fuel Production

Prior to the late 1940s, the Gulf Coast states of the United States exported large quantities of oil to Western Europe. But by 1950, rapidly expanding exports from lower-cost Persian Gulf sources had nearly driven American oil out of European markets; the United States had even begun to import small amounts of this Persian Gulf oil. The now familiar "national security" argument began with these early Middle East shipments. It held that dependence on oil imports was dangerous because their flow might be interrupted and such interruptions would cause economic havoc; therefore, the United States should adopt policies that would either limit its dependence on oil imports or create ready reserves. Throughout the 1950s and early 1960s, this argument was used to rationalize the adoption of oil-import quotas, the continuation of the oil depletion allowance, and the creation of other energy policies aimed at protecting national security, which at that time was in no apparent danger.

The national security justification was generally inappropriate until well into the 1960s. The United States imported relatively little oil, and virtually all that it did import came from Canadian or Caribbean sources. Prior to 1970, prolonged interruptions from either source were unlikely. Moreover, if an interruption had occurred, the United States felt that there was spare domestic capacity that could be tapped. But around 1970, a rapid deterioration in United States oil security occurred. Two factors precipitated this decline.

First, United States consumption of foreign oil grew at a 30 percent annual rate between 1970 and 1973 (from 3.4 million to 6.2 million barrels per day). Second, the OPEC nations succeeded in increasing their monopoly power as their customers capitulated to repeated demands for higher prices.

The United States' domestic crude oil production, which peaked at an average of 9.6 million barrels per day in 1970, has been falling steadily ever since. By 1975, its crude oil production had fallen to 8.2 million barrels per day. At the same time, the growth rate of consumption accelerated, primarily because (1) there was a natural gas shortage, (2) electric utilities had to substitute residual fuel oil for coal in order to comply with new stationary source air emission standards, and (3) the engines produced by automobile manufacturers, in their efforts to comply with motor vehicle emission standards, were less efficient (used more gasoline) than earlier engines. As a result, the United States was increasingly dependent on foreign oil.

The OPEC nations had formed their cartel, in 1960, for the explicit purpose of preventing world oil prices from falling. But throughout the 1960s, world oil supplies grew faster than demand. Estimated crude oil prices (at the Persian Gulf) fell from about $1.70–$1.90 per barrel in 1960 to $1.20–$1.40 in early 1970. Not until the early 1970s did the world's surplus oil capacity begin to disappear:

> The stage was set by the closing of the Suez Canal in the 1967 war and a consequent tanker shortage brought on by the elongated haul around the Cape of Good Hope. Then in May 1970, Tapline, normally capable of bringing half a million barrels a day of Saudi oil to the Mediterranean, was cut by a bulldozer accident in Syria, and the Syrian government claimed that conditions were too turbulent . . . for a repair team to work. . . . Nigeria was torn by civil war. The new revolutionary Libyan government, claiming to be displeased with the conservation practices of the oil producers, ordered production cutbacks totalling approximately 400,000 barrels daily. The Libyans concurrently demanded improved terms from the oil companies. With tanker rates sky-high, Libyan oil was selling at a substantial premium, and the Libyans were demanding a modest

share of that premium. In September 1970, the Libyan government won a $0.30 increase in the posted price and an increase in the tax rate from 50 to between 54 and 58 percent.

In December 1970, Venezuela unilaterally increased its tax rate from 52 to 60 percent. The Persian Gulf producers, witnessing the Venezuelan and Libyan triumphs, demanded more. . . .

After an extensive and stormy process of negotiations, an agreement was reached in February 1971 in Tehran . . . raising the posted price by $0.35, with an additional $0.11 annual escalation through 1975. . . .

The Libyans then announced that if the Persian Gulf countries got more, they, the Libyans, should receive still more. . . .

The oil companies wanted to preclude leapfrogging by jointly negotiating a single contractual rate with OPEC. . . .

But even if the leapfrogging had been halted, the fundamental change that underlay the oil revolution could not have been avoided. For the first time, the OPEC countries, particularly the Persian Gulf producers, demonstrated their readiness to restrict output. The resulting bargaining strength, rather than any supply shortage in 1970, explains the 1971 and subsequent OPEC successes.[1]

In 1971, when the claims of the domestic oil producers finally came true, they had spent 20 years invoking national security in the absence of a real oil security threat. Like the boy who cried "Wolf!" they had exhausted their credibility. Few policymakers perceived a threat in OPEC's actions until the October 1973 embargo by its Arab members.

Guaranteeing oil security is of immediate concern to all oil-importing nations. A significant longer-term question is whether the world's energy supplies will be adequate to meet future demands. This question was raised in 1972 by the Club of Rome with the publication of *The Limits of Growth*.[2] This volume rekindled interest in the Malthusian proposition that future energy supplies will be inadequate to meet growing demands. It contends that

1. The world's physical supplies of the energy resources necessary to support all physiological and industrial activity are finite.
2. The demand for these resources has grown throughout recorded history and will continue to grow.
3. Therefore, the world's energy demands will someday exhaust physical supplies.

Most economists have rejected this syllogism, drawing a distinction between ultimate energy reserves and commercial energy reserves. The world's ultimate energy supply is essentially infinite. But at any time, the planet's known commercial energy reserves are the product of past exploration and development, present technology, current energy prices, and projections of future energy prices. Barring contrary government policies, whenever energy consumption seems likely to exhaust commercial supplies, energy prices will rise. The price increase will give consumers an incentive to reduce consumption and give producers an incentive to find, develop, and produce new—previously undiscovered or unprofitable—energy supplies. Energy prices will continue to rise until a new balance is struck between supply and demand. Therefore the key question is not whether world energy supplies will be adequate over the foreseeable future but how much adequate supplies will cost.

PROJECT INDEPENDENCE

On November 7, 1973, President Nixon announced Project Independence. Its goal was to enable the United States to meet its energy needs "without depending on any foreign energy sources"[3] by 1980. This announcement, intended as a prompt and vigorous response to the OPEC embargo, preceded efforts by the President's advisers to familiarize themselves with the facts concerning the nation's energy needs, domestic reserves, and production capacity. Subsequently, they learned that they had underestimated the time it would take to introduce and gain widespread acceptance of energy-saving consumer durables and capital goods. They found that the United States could not move rapidly to curtail energy demands without immediately halting the growth of the GNP and guaranteeing economic recessions and stagnation throughout the remainder of the 1970s. They also found it difficult to step up domestic production of the four most important primary fuels (oil, gas, coal, and nuclear). And they learned that significant commercial production of less conventional fuels, such as shale oil, geothermal power, and coal synthetics, was at least 15 years away. As a result, the goals of Project Independence have changed several times.

In November 1974, the FEA, an agency that administers oil price and allocation regulations, completed *The Project Independence Report,* a massive study evaluating the United States' prospects for achieving "energy independence" by 1985.[4] Representatives of both industry and academe praised the report as a first attempt to assess available facts for policy evaluation. But they criticized its specific projections of domestic production of the four major types of energy—crude oil, natural gas, coal, and nuclear power—as overly optimistic.[5] In 1976, the FEA took account of this criticism when it released *The National Energy Outlook,*[6] a report whose projections of United States energy production in 1985 are lower than those of the 1974 report for all categories of fuel (see Table 3). Nevertheless, the FEA continues to project large increases (above 1976 levels) in domestic output of most fuels.

The levels of energy consumption and supply of the United States in 1985 depend in large part on unpredictable economic, political, technical, and geological conditions, such as the nation's economic growth rate, the actual effects of policies intended to stimulate domestic fuel production and encourage greater conservation, and the success of the OPEC cartel in maintaining and using its monopoly power. But in any case, large new reserves must be discovered and developed if domestic energy production is to grow—or at least not decline. And expanded domestic fuel production is essential to the policy goals of energy availability and energy security.

The government must take an active role in developing adequate supplies of domestic energy because more than half of the nation's untapped supplies of the four most

Table 3   The FEA's Reference Case Projections of the U.S. 1985 Energy Consumption by Fuel Source

FUEL	1974 PROJECTIONS*	1976 PROJECTIONS†
	(QUADRILLION BTU)	
Coal	22.9	20.6
Crude oil	31.3	27.8
Natural gas	24.8	22.8
Nuclear	12.5	8.7
Oil and gas imports	6.5	15.1
Other	4.8	3.9
Total	102.8	98.9

Source: Federal Energy Administration, *Project Independence Report* (Washington, D.C.: U.S. Government Printing Office, 1974), p. 46.

†*Source:* Federal Energy Administration, *National Energy Outlook, 1976* (Washington, D.C.: U.S. Government Printing Office, 1976), pp. 16, 39, and 131. The entries in this column assume that 1 quadrillion Btu are contained in 182.5 million barrels of crude oil or in 0.97 trillion cubic feet of natural gas.

widely used fuels appear to be located on federally owned lands. The federal government owns the entire Outer Continental Shelf and most of northern Alaska—the two areas considered the most promising sources of future United States oil and natural gas supplies. In addition, it owns most of the still largely undeveloped Western coal and uranium lands. But even the most vigorous efforts to stimulate production face a variety of constraints that raise serious questions about the plausibility of the most recent FEA projections.

CRUDE OIL

Since peaking at 3.5 billion barrels (9.6 million barrels per day) in 1970, crude oil production in the United States has been falling at a steady annual rate of about 3 percent. It dropped to about 3 billion barrels (8.2 million barrels per day) in 1975 and was still falling in early 1976. This decline will be reversed temporarily in late 1977 when Prudhoe Bay's oil begins to flow south through the Alaskan pipeline. But the fall is certain to resume in the early 1980s unless United States producers discover and develop large new crude oil reserves. Debate now flourishes over whether the United States has sufficient undiscovered but ultimately recoverable crude oil reserves to sustain a sizable expansion of output.

The total resource cost of producing crude oil (or natural gas) includes all exploration, development, and operating expenses. Exploration costs are incurred in the search for oil in areas where its presence is suspected but has not yet been confirmed. Development costs pay for the facilities (e.g., wells, gathering lines, etc.) necessary to provide access to previously discovered petroleum reserves. Operating costs pay for the actual extraction of crude oil from its natural sources.

The geological characteristics of oil and gas fields in different parts of the world vary enormously. For example, the oil fields of the Persian Gulf are unusually large, numerous, and productive; hence, the total resource cost of a typical new barrel of this region's oil is only about 35 cents.[7] But much of the new oil to be produced in the United States will come from small, scattered, geographically isolated, or low-yield fields that can produce oil only at a resource cost of more than $10 per barrel.

Differences in size, number, location, and productivity of crude oil fields account not only for large regional variations in resource costs but also for large regional variations in the speed with which output can increase. For example, huge, geographically accessible, but largely undeveloped reserves of low-cost crude oil have already been discovered in several Persian Gulf countries; producers can expand output substantially in these areas merely by drilling a relatively few additional wells and installing the appropriate surface gathering and storage facilities. Within only a year or two after producers decide to raise future crude oil production capacity, significant quantities of new output can come on stream.

In the United States, on the other hand, producers do not know of many large and geographically accessible oil fields with commercial potential. Hence, they must incur higher exploration costs to produce a given quantity of new oil than must producers in the Middle East, and this exploration usually takes several years. In 1975, only one out of every five wildcat wells drilled in the United States hit either oil or gas.

The development of already discovered commercial reserves also takes longer in the United States than in the Persian Gulf and involves the use of more extensive development facilities because United States oil fields tend to be much smaller and less productive. (A large Persian Gulf field may have recoverable reserves of 10 billion barrels or more, and individual wells frequently produce more than 10,000 barrels per day. A large United States oil field contains only 100 million barrels of recoverable reserves, and an outstanding well typically produces only 100 to 500 barrels per day.) Thus, the process of raising crude oil output substantially above currently planned levels will take at least 3 to 6 years in the Gulf of Mexico and up to 10 years in less accessible frontier areas, such as the Alaskan North Slope.

Most of the crude oil already produced in the United States has come from a few large fields. According to a recent study for the Environmental Protection Agency:

> 250 of the 60,000 odd reservoirs in the United States account for over 65 percent of domestic production to date, 75 percent of . . . recoverable reserves and over 60 percent of the already discovered remaining oil in place. And, even within this sample of large fields, the distribution of volume is highly skewed toward the 100 largest fields.[8]

The oil industry drills the best prospects first. Hence, between 1860 and 1920, United States onshore oil exploration produced an average of 240 barrels per foot drilled, whereas in recent years, exploration has yielded only 20 to 30 barrels per foot drilled. Except for the Alaskan North Slope and large areas of the Outer Continental Shelf, most areas of the United States that are considered likely to have commercial quantities of petroleum have already been heavily explored. And because large fields tend to be easier to find than small ones, most of the larger and more productive fields in these heavily explored areas have almost certainly been discovered and developed and most of those not already exhausted are now being worked. (Of course, a few large fields, notably the Jay Field and

Hatters Pond, have been discovered in onshore areas of the 48 contiguous states within the past 10 years.) These facts suggest that, even though the United States has increased petroleum exploration and development efforts at a 17 percent annual rate in the three years since the OAPEC embargo, the United States will find it difficult to reverse the post-1970 decline in onshore crude oil output in the contiguous 48 states.[9]

ALASKA AND THE CONTINENTAL SHELF

The most promising locations for domestic oil prospecters currently are the unexplored areas of the Alaskan North Slope and the Outer Continental Shelf. Prudhoe Bay on the Alaskan North Slope is by far the largest and most productive oil field ever discovered in North America. Discovered by Atlantic-Richfield and Exxon in 1968, it has proved reserves of 9.6 billion barrels. Prudhoe Bay's principal owners (Atlantic-Richfield, Exxon, and Standard Oil of Ohio) expect it to produce roughly 1.6 million barrels per day—nearly 20 percent of United States 1975 total crude oil output—in the early 1980s.

Normally, a large discovery such as Prudhoe Bay would have precipitated a "black gold rush" in promising nearby geological formations. In 1969, Alaska leased nearby state lands for $900 million, and exploratory activity surged briefly. This exploration proved disappointing. Further exploration has been hampered by Alaska's failure to lease additional land and by the federal government's delay in authorizing sufficient funds to explore systematically U.S. Naval Petroleum Reservation No. 4 (NPR No. 4), a 24-million-acre site almost bordering the Prudhoe Bay field. North Slope exploration also has been delayed indirectly by the environmental litigation that held up authorization of construction of the trans-Alaskan pipeline for four years. Although in the end the environmentalists lost their case, they made oil companies hesitate to undertake additional exploration investments. Today—eight years after the enormous Prudhoe Bay discovery—all estimates of the Alaskan North Slope's petroleum potential remain quite speculative, and none of its oil has been delivered to United States markets.

Oil from the Outer Continental Shelf has been produced commercially since the late 1940s. By United States standards, the OCS fields currently in production are relatively large, and their production costs, excluding lease bonus payments, are relatively low.[10] Between 1970 and 1975, the federal government held 12 large and 3 small OCS lease sales involving about 6 million acres for which companies paid the U.S. Treasury more than $12 billion in bonuses. But exploring and developing new land takes time; hence, most of the offshore oil produced during 1975 (about 1.5 million barrels per day) came from portions of 7 million acres of federally owned OCS lands leased prior to 1970. Most of the rest came from state-owned lands. The OCS acreage leased since 1970 is just beginning to produce significant quantities of crude oil and natural gas. If the oil companies are to recover their mammoth post-1970 leasing investments, production from these recently leased OCS areas will have to exceed more than 1 million barrels of crude oil (or natural gas equivalents) per day when they are fully operating.[11]

The Interior Department has announced its intention to continue leasing large areas of OCS lands at least until 1980. Despite state and private objections, the federal government is planning large lease sales both in the Gulf of Alaska and off the Atlantic coast. (The first Atlantic sale was held in August 1976.) But most of the land to be leased is in the traditional areas of United States offshore production—the Gulf of Mexico and California coastal waters at depths of less than 200 meters. As of January 1976, the United States still had not leased roughly 77 million acres of these OCS lands. The Gulf and California coastal waters contain another 160 million unleased acres at depths of between 200 and 2,500 meters, but very few areas beyond 200 meters deep have been leased. Academic, industry, and government geologists all agree that, because the most promising acreage in traditional OCS waters has already been explored, the remainder is unlikely to contain sufficient reserves to reverse the present decline in U.S. crude oil output.[12]

The Atlantic coastal waters, the Gulf of Alaska (off southern Alaska), and the Beaufort Sea (off northern Alaska) are the areas of the OCS now thought most likely to hold significant new oil reserves for expanding the United States' domestic production. However, since drilling is just beginning in the virgin OCS lands, this assessment is based on untested inferences from geological and geophysical data. In the early 1970s, a number of companies used these methods to identify several large natural gas formations in the western Gulf of Mexico. Preliminary geophysical studies suggest that the OCS waters of the Gulf of Alaska and the Atlantic seaboard may contain oil-bearing structures that are larger and less complex than those in the Gulf of Mexico.[13]

Unfortunately, geophysical techniques are not foolproof. In 1973, prompted by promising geophysical surveys, an Exxon-led consortium paid the U.S. Treasury a record $632.4 million bonus to lease just six tracts on the Destin anticline in the previously undrilled eastern Gulf of Mexico. Seven dry wildcats and an additional $15 million later, the three companies in this consortium abandoned drilling. The Destin debacle illustrates the need for some drilling as a prerequisite to an informed estimate of an area's petroleum potential.

It would be exceedingly useful for energy policymakers to have better information about the petroleum potential of the frontier OCS lands—knowledge they can acquire only through exploration and preliminary drilling. But before exploration begins, they must determine (1) whether and how much to compensate the coastal states; (2) whether the private sector or government itself should undertake OCS exploration, development, and production; and (3) if private firms handle all stages of oil production, how the government can derive the most financial benefit from leasing its lands without delaying the pace of production or causing production inefficiencies. Once these issues are resolved, initial drilling may then reveal that the frontier OCS lands are not very promising sources of oil. In that event, energy policymakers will have to choose between increased reliance on imported oil and concerted efforts either to reduce demand or to accelerate development of other kinds of energy.

On the other hand, if some of the previously unexplored

OCS lands do have oil, policymakers must weigh such possible consequences of expanded OCS development as social disruption in small towns suddenly flooded with oil workers and oil wealth and environmental damage from accidental oil spills.

Large-scale crude oil production in the Outer Continental Shelf will result inevitably in some large spills. In 1973, a group of experts estimated that maintenance of present OCS production would result in an average of two major drilling blowouts and two major production accidents each year.[14] Their study also concluded:

> Assuming that present drilling procedures and technologies are used in the future, the rate of serious accidents will probably remain essentially constant, with evolutionary improvements in equipment and procedures being balanced by a move into deep water and more hostile environments.[15]

Another report describes the effects of a 1969 tanker spill of refined oil products off West Falmouth, Massachusetts:

> Massive, immediate destruction of marine life occurred offshore during the first few days after the accident. Affected were a wide range of fish, shellfish, worms, crabs and other crustaceans, and invertebrates. . . . Trawls made in ten feet of water soon after the spill showed that 95% of the animals recovered were dead. . . . Our investigation demonstrated that the spill produced . . . destruction of fishery resources and continued harm to fisheries for a long period after the accident.[16]

Large oil spills can cause considerable biological and esthetic damage if they reach intertidal areas. But most OCS production platforms are many miles from shore, and crude oil is less toxic and more biodegradable than the refined oil products that were spilled near West Falmouth.

Present methods of cleaning up spills include using mechanical skimmers, absorbents, containment booms, chemical dispersants, sinking agents, and burning. They are ineffective in rough seas and take too much time to implement when spills take place in the ecologically fragile intertidal area.[17] Cleanup technology is improving, but great improvements appear unlikely in the near future.

A decision to encourage OCS oil production should include an extensive resource commitment for the prevention of oil spills, including more vigilant regulation, inspection, and detection capabilities; improved training of production personnel; and tighter specifications for OCS production platforms. But decision makers should not restrict their consideration to the environmental hazards posed by future OCS activity; they must consider also the environmental costs of the alternatives.

The only feasible alternative to OCS oil, at least through 1985, is oil imports delivered by tanker. But tanker accidents are much more likely to cause oil spills, and those spills are likely to happen more often and do more harm than those from OCS production.[18] Tanker accidents are most likely to occur near ports, where shipping lanes are most congested and a spill is most damaging, and tankers often carry refined petroleum products, which are both more toxic and less biodegradable than crude oil. Kenneth O. Emery, Henry Briant Bigelow Oceanographer at the Woods Hole Oceanographic Institution, recently noted:

> The environmental outcry has occurred mainly because of the increasing presence of tar on beaches and the death of shore birds from oil spills. While the Santa Barbara oil spill catalyzed the rise of environmentalism, only three wells and one pipeline accident, from more than 18,000 wells drilled on our continental shelves, have spilled more than 1,000 tons of oil each since 1953. This is a safety factor of 99.978 per unit at this level. In contrast, tanker operations spill about 20 times as much oil annually as does oil production from the world's continental shelves. This ratio is being reduced by increased use of load-on-top tankers, but simultaneously some of the huge tankers needed for economic long-distance transportation of oil . . . are becoming old and tired, with increased danger of breaking apart at sea. Thus, we who are interested in preserving the environment should favor increased oil production

from the United States' shelves rather than from long-distance-tanker importation.[19]

Although oil produced from the Alaskan Gulf may pose special problems, higher production from other United States coastal waters seems likely to pose fewer environmental hazards than higher oil imports.[20]

Table 4 presents the *National Energy Outlook* projections of United States crude oil production in 1985 by source. The accuracy of these projections depends on the validity of underlying assumptions regarding (1) future oil price levels and the effect of price on output; (2) the size, location, and timing of future sales of federal oil land leases; and (3) the true crude oil potential of unexplored areas—in particular, the Alaskan North Slope and the virgin waters of the Outer Continental Shelf. These assumptions are all highly conjectural. For example, domestic oil prices (adjusted for inflation) may never reach the $13 per barrel level assumed by the FEA. (Indeed, the Energy Policy and Conservation Act of 1975 initially rolled back domestic crude oil prices to an average of only $7.66 per barrel.) Moreover, econometric estimates of the price-elasticity (i.e., responsiveness) of United States crude oil supplies differ substantially and have been known to be wide of the mark. And given the difference between pre- and post-OAPEC-embargo oil prices, statistical relationships deduced from preembargo data have no necessary bearing on the future. Furthermore, recent history suggests that the Interior Department will revise its OCS leasing plans in response to judicial decisions and other constraints. And even if leasing and exploration proceed at maximum speed, the true extent of United States petroleum reserves will still be unknown for some years to come.

Without more solid data and without knowledge of policy choices yet to be made by the federal government, all attempts to project the level of United States oil supplies more than three to five years into the future must be viewed skeptically. But the United States' 1985 crude oil output seems unlikely to be less than 9 million or more than 13 million barrels per day. (The FEA projects a range of between 10.1 million and 16.1 million barrels per day.[21]) If the recent fall in onshore output in the 48 contiguous states cannot be halted in the near future

Table 4   FEA Estimates of 1985 U.S. Crude Oil Production Assuming a $13 per Barrel Price

(MILLION BARRELS PER DAY)

Lower 48 Onshore	
New field primary/secondary	1.9
Old field secondary	2.0
Tertiary	1.0
Initial reserves	2.4
Subtotal	7.3
Lower 48 OCS	
Pacific	0.6
Gulf of Mexico	1.4
Atlantic	0.1
Subtotal	2.1
Alaska	
Beaufort Sea	0.4
Other OCS	0.4
North Slope	2.3
NPR No. 4	—
Subtotal	3.1
Other	
NPR No. 1	0.2
Tar sands	—
Heavy hydrocarbons	0.2
Subtotal	0.4
Total crude	12.9
Natural gas liquids	1.9
Total liquids	14.8

Source: Federal Energy Administration, *National Energy Outlook, 1976,* Table II-3, p. 64.

and if exploration of virgin areas is either delayed or proves unsuccessful, the United States' crude oil output in 1985 will be near the lower end of this range.

NATURAL GAS

The production and consumption of natural gas place less stress on the environment than do the production and consumption of most other types of energy now commercially available: the combustion of natural gas is nearly pollution-free, and leaked natural gas usually dissipates quickly and harmlessly into the atmosphere. Apart from its use for home and industrial heating, natural gas is prized as a raw material for petrochemicals and as a fuel for certain high-tolerance industrial processes such as the manufacture of curved and shatter-resistant automobile-window shields. Since 1968, natural gas reserves have not grown sufficiently to prevent a decline in production that is likely to continue for several years (see Table 5). Since 1 trillion cubic feet of natural gas are equivalent to roughly 0.5 million barrels of crude oil, a substantial fall in natural gas production implies a substantial rise in United States oil imports.

Natural gas is usually found in geological formations like those that contain crude oil, and the production technology is roughly the same for both fuels. Hence, the same economic, geological, and technical conditions that affect crude oil production also affect natural gas production. The price-responsiveness of supply is equally difficult to assess for both fuels.

The FEA projects that natural gas production might rise to 22.3 trillion cubic feet by 1985 if prices of interstate natural

Table 5   Projected Near-Term Deliveries of Natural Gas to Interstate Pipelines

	PROJECTED DELIVERIES					
	1974	*1975*	*1976*	*1977*	*1978*	*1979*
	(BILLION CUBIC FEET PER YEAR)					
Domestic gas supply	12,965	11,824	10,844	9,807	8,753	7,803
Pipeline imports	900	922	927	930	932	933
Liquid natural gas imports	0	0	0	146	332	360
Totals	13,866	12,746	11,772	10,833	10,016	9,097

Source: Federal Energy Administration, *National Energy Outlook, 1976,* Table III-6, p. 127.

gas were deregulated and allowed to rise from a present average of about 40 cents to about $2 per thousand cubic feet (mcf). The FEA's projections for a variety of other scenarios range between 17.0 trillion and 25.3 trillion cubic feet.[22] Substantially higher natural gas prices do appear necessary if the fall in United States gas production is to be reversed. But although higher prices would stimulate natural gas production, their effects would not become apparent for some time. Moreover, in view of leasing schedule delays and uncertainties and geological unknowns, the FEA projection of 1985 United States natural gas production, assuming that prices are deregulated, probably represents a maximum.

COAL

Coal is abundant in the United States, but its share of the energy market has fallen steadily since 1900.[23] Certainly, increased use of coal can help to alleviate United States reliance on foreign petroleum. Nevertheless, until recently the use of coal was declining because its users had to maintain large and dirty on-site storage facilities and cheap fuel oil and natural as were frequently available. Coal is much less versatile than natural gas and refined oil products. Ninety percent of all the coal produced is consumed by just two large users—electric utilities and metal smelters—and no coal has been used in the transportation sector since the steam locomotive became obsolete. Unless the production of synthetic natural gas or oil from coal becomes commercially feasible, coal can replace petroleum in large quantities only for electricity generation and large industrial uses.

The mining and combustion of coal pose difficult environmental problems. Coal combustion emits more pollutants—especially sulphur oxides, but also particulates—than the combustion of the other fossil fuels. The use of stack gas scrubbers and low-sulphur coal can eliminate many of these pollutants, but many utilities complain that stack gas scrubbers are expensive to install and maintain and often do not work. Low-sulphur coal is in short supply east of the

Mississippi.[24] Although the western part of the United States contains large reserves of low-sulphur coal, they are located far from markets and have a relatively low energy content. Hence, the transportation costs of using such coal would be high. Present proposals call for this coal to be shipped directly south, west, and east via unit trains or coal slurry pipelines or, prior to shipment, transformed into electricity or synthetic coal derivatives in giant plants built near the mine mouth.

Because of the relative thickness of known coal seams and the comparatively shallow overburden, nearly all Western coal will be strip-mined. The extent of the damage caused by strip mining depends upon the magnitude of postmining reclamation efforts. The success of these efforts depends on slope height and angle, water supply, soil conditions, and the methods used in stripping, storing, and returning the overburden to the site.

In the Midwest, for example, high levels of rainfall and reasonably flat terrain facilitate reclamation. (Unfortunately, much of this coal has a high sulphur content.) Although the northern Great Plains are flat, they also are dry. Nearly 40 percent of this region's coal reserves lies in areas that receive less than 10 inches of rainfall per year, much less than is normally required to restore a strip-mining site. The remaining 60 percent of Western coal lies in areas where reclamation will be difficult and expensive but apparently feasible given current coal prices.

The processing of coal to produce electricity or to be converted into synthetic gas or oil uses large quantities of water as a coolant and processing agent. The indigenous water supplies in the northern Great Plains may be too low for these purposes. If so, either local processing plants will have to bring in water diverted from other regions (perhaps Canada) or Western coal will have to be shipped directly to the nation's major fuel-consuming centers.

In short, the United States will face significant problems as it tries to expand its production and consumption of coal. But domestic reserves of coal are much more abundant than domestic reserves of crude oil and natural gas, and coal is much cheaper (per Btu) to produce. Hence, coal producers can make substantial investments to overcome coal's unique pollution problems without pricing themselves out of the market. Of course, because such investments yield no direct commercial benefits, producers are unlikely to make them unless encouraged by appropriate government policies.

Table 3 presents the FEA's 1976 projections of the United States coal consumption in 1985. If the government adopts policies in the near future to facilitate strip mining and leasing of Western coal lands, these projections seem plausible.

NUCLEAR FUELS

From a commercial standpoint, nuclear fuels are even less flexible than coal. Their sole important commercial use is to generate electricity. At the end of 1975, fifty-six commercial nuclear reactors, with a combined capacity of 35,000 megawatts, were operating in the United States. These plants accounted for approximately 7 percent of the nation's total electricity-generating capacity.[25]

Efforts to expand nuclear electricity-generating capacity raise a number of public health and safety questions: How safe are nuclear reactors? Can nuclear wastes be safely stored and transported? What are the dangers of nuclear proliferation, theft, and blackmail? What risks are tolerable?

The safety record of the nuclear reactors currently in operation is excellent. None has ever leaked significant amounts of radioactive materials, and the few commercial reactor accidents that have occurred have caused no fatalities.[26] But given the extreme and prolonged toxicity of radioactive substances, policymakers must assess the probability of a major reactor accident, the extent of the damage it might cause, and the public's willingness to tolerate the risks it perceives to be associated with nuclear power expansion.

The most serious technical risk posed by the presence of a nuclear reactor is that of a "loss-of-coolant" accident. If a reactor's core is not adequately cooled, its nuclear fuel may melt down, breach the walls of the steel and concrete containment vessel, and release radioactive materials into the environment. Nuclear reactors are designed to keep their cores adequately cooled; a loss-of-coolant accident could occur only if both primary and emergency core-cooling systems failed. If both of these systems did in fact fail, local topographical and weather conditions would determine the speed and the ultimate extent of dispersion of radioactive substances.

The Atomic Energy Commission (AEC) (as well as its successor, the Nuclear Regulatory Commission) has sponsored numerous assessments of the dangers posed by loss-of-coolant accidents. All of these studies have concluded that the probability of a simultaneous failure of both coolant systems is infinitesimal; most have concluded that if, nevertheless, such an accident did occur, it would cause fewer than 300 fatalities. But some unofficial estimates of the fatalities that might result from a meltdown accident run as high as 45,000.[27]

The most extensive AEC-sponsored reactor accident assessment study—know as "WASH-1400"—estimates the probability of a core melt as 1 in 20,000 per reactor per year.[28] Assuming that 100 nuclear plants are in operation, WASH-1400 reports that a nuclear accident resulting in 10 or more fatalities is likely to occur once every 3,000 years; an accident killing 1,000-plus citizens is likely only once in 100,000 years; the largest number of possible deaths reported in the study is 3,300.[29]

Because actual accident data are virtually nonexistent, the WASH-1400 probability estimates are based largely on computer simulations. But a recent incident has raised questions about the estimates' validity. In March 1975, an electrician using a candle to check insulation started a fire that forced the Tennessee Valley Authority (TVA) to shut down the two giant reactors at its power plant near Athens, Alabama. One reactor was shut down without incident; the other began to lose coolant and overheat. When TVA personnel attempted to activate the emergency core-cooling system, they found that a power failure caused by the fire had rendered it inoperable. Fortunately, the operating engineers were able to connect auxiliary pumps by hand in time to flood the core with water and prevent a meltdown.[30]

A study of a draft version of WASH-1400 (chaired by Professor Harold Lewis, jointly sponsored by the National Science Foundation and the Energy Research and Development Administration, and published by the American Physical Society in midsummer 1975) concludes, "We have not uncovered reasons for substantial short-range consideration regarding risk of accidents in light water reactors."[31] Although it points out that "quantification of biological effects following radiation exposure is a subject full of uncertainties," its estimates of fatalities, genetic defects, and other damage that might result from a reactor accident are roughly 25 times higher than those in draft WASH-1400.[32]

Another public health and safety issue facing the nuclear power industry is the disposition of nuclear wastes, which remain highly toxic for periods ranging from several centuries for strontium 90 and cesium 137 to 250,000 years for plutonium. Most of those who favor a nuclear moratorium maintain that no technology exists for either dissipating the effects of nuclear wastes or storing them safely. Of course, the more reactors we build in the short run, the more imperative it becomes to find a permanent solution to the waste problem in the long run.

Some experts believe that recently developed procedures for drying the wastes and molding them into a ceramic that can be encased in steel and buried show promise of providing a permanent technical solution to the nuclear waste storage problem.[33]

A higher-priority concern may center on the problems of transporting nuclear wastes (or fuels) both safely and securely. The risks that some terrorist organization may steal substantial amounts of waste or sabotage reactors are probably impossible to evaluate. They may be high. The fact that a student was able to design a primitive but possibly workable atomic bomb, combined with the steady accretion of nuclear materials and the flagrant determination of a new generation of terrorists, suggests grave possibilities. But other methods of causing mass deaths are much more readily available to the committed terrorist. And as the science editor of the *Christian Science Monitor* noted in a recent article, nuclear experts are devising some very sophisticated deterrents to the potential terrorist threat.[34] Nevertheless, the public fear of nuclear sabotage or terrorism is far from being allayed.

Any country possessing a nuclear power plant has the potential to develop limited nuclear weapons capability, as India's 1974 explosion of an atomic bomb fueled by plutonium from its small Canadian-built research reactor demonstrates. It is already too late to stop nuclear proliferation unless all countries that are major suppliers of nuclear reactors and reprocessing plants cooperate for this purpose.

The issue of whether to expand nuclear generating capacity is exceedingly complex. Reputable scientists—garnering information on all we know about the effects of radiation, the precautionary design features of reactors, security systems, safety records, and other pertinent data—have ascribed a relatively low risk to nuclear reactors. Nevertheless, the following excerpt from a recent *New York Times* article by the respected science writer, Robert Gillette, summarizes some widespread fears:

> Nuclear power by any measure is an awesome technology. ... Yet for some, awe gives way to a deeply felt fear that, where a modern, 1,000-million-watt atomic plant is concerned, simple and perhaps inevitable human error may lead to catastrophe. Such would seem to be the case for Dale Bridenbaugh, Richard Hubbard and Gregory Minor, the engineers who recently quit their jobs at General Electric's nuclear division—and for Robert D. Pollard, one of the Federal Nuclear Regulatory Commission's 48 project managers who followed suit a few days later.
>
> These four engineers were not the first, and they are probably not the last, to renounce promising careers to tell the public that nuclear power is unsafe, or at any rate not safe enough. ...
>
> What is the public to make of these acts of technological apostasy?

A cynic might say that jeopardizing one's job security may testify to a man's sincerity but not necessarily to his prescience. Yet there is no disputing that 30 years into the nuclear age this once-promising technology remains burdened with a host of unresolved problems. Mr. Pollard and the three General Electric engineers invoked the leading ones in explaining their public resignations: What to do with nuclear waste that remains lethal for centuries? How to mitigate the risks of theft and sabotage in a plutonium economy? And, most important, how to settle the scores of engineering questions that still cloud the day-to-day operation of the nation's 57 licensed nuclear power reactors?

Although some progress has been made in calculating the real risks involved in these problems, their urgency is still a matter of subjective engineering judgment: The best that can be said is that honest engineers disagree wildly.[35]

These vociferously aired disputes within the scientific community have fortified public suspicion that the concerned government agencies are either incapable of ferreting out the truth or, perhaps, even responsible for suppressing it. In such conditions, sound policymaking is exceedingly difficult.

In 1974, the FEA projected that, by 1985, the United States would increase its nuclear-powered electricity-generating capacity by about 170,000 megawatts.[36] In 1976, the FEA projected that nuclear capacity would expand 105,000 megawatts by 1985.[37] The agency reduced its estimate as a result of the post-1973 decision by electric utilities to abandon or delay building roughly 141,000 megawatts of new nuclear capacity because of falling electricity demands, rising construction and financing costs, and growing opposition by nuclear power critics. To make even the lower projection a reality without substantially increasing reliance on uranium imports, the United States will have to accelerate its exploration and development of new uranium sources and enhance its capacity to enrich these ores. A great deal is still to be learned about the size of the domestic (and foreign) uranium resource base and the economics and technical feasibility of its commercial production. But the available data do not contradict the FEA's more recent projections.

OTHER PRIMARY FUELS

The OAPEC embargo produced a burst of enthusiasm for the development of such energy sources as oil shale, tar sands, synthetic coal derivatives, geothermal power, solar power, and fusion. Subsequently, it became apparent that, whatever their ultimate importance or potential, and whatever policies government may adopt, prior to 1985 these sources will provide only trivial increments to United States energy supplies.

Between 1958 and 1973, government and corporate officials maintained that oil shale would become competitive with domestic crude oil if the latter were priced only slightly higher than it then was. In the early 1970s, when oil prices began rising sharply, several producers announced plans to develop oil shale plants capable of producing 50,000 to 100,000 barrels per day of crude oil equivalents. But by 1975, the capital cost estimates for these oil shale plants had more than doubled, reaching over $1 billion; as a result, several large oil companies, including Atlantic-Richfield, Shell, and The Oil Shale Corporation, abandoned these plans. It is now evident that, unless producers receive hefty subsidies or devise significant cost-cutting innovations, oil shale cannot compete with crude oil selling at $12 to $14 per barrel. Similarly, the available commercial technology for coal gasification produces a product that is roughly twice as expensive as imported crude oil. And Federal Power Commission rules that mandate that all of the economic benefits of lower costs must be passed on to the consumer have discouraged the development of a cheaper coal-gasification technology. Commercial processes for coal liquefaction have yet to be demonstrated.

Environmental problems as well as technological and economic problems surround the production of oil shale and tar sands. At present, shale oil can be produced commercially only if the shale rock is strip-mined and then heated in huge retorts to extract the oil. Because only a small portion of the shale is actually oil, transportation costs are prohibitive; thus, retorts must be located near the mine. Most of the United

States' extensive reserves of oil shale are located in mountainous areas whose water supplies appear to be inadequate to support both large-scale mining and retorting, let alone reclamation. "Spent shale," the waste residual after extraction and retorting, occupies some 15 percent more volume than in-place shale rock and is sterile. Satisfactory methods of disposing of this apparently useless material have yet to be devised.

A sustained, controlled nuclear fusion reaction has yet to be achieved. And even after a breakthrough, fusion power is unlikely to become commercial for at least 25 more years.

Most undeveloped domestic geothermal sources are poisoned with corrosive salts. No commercial technology exists for using corrosive steams to generate electricity. Solar energy is very diffuse, and the known techniques for collecting it in large quantities are prohibitively expensive.

ELECTRICITY

Although electricity is not a primary fuel source, it has special importance because coal and nuclear power, as well as longer-range exotic sources, can be consumed in large quantities only if their energy is first converted into electricity. Electricity also is a flexible, convenient form of energy. Until the late 1960s, economies of scale and technological progress caused electric rates to fall relative to other fuel prices. From the mid-1930s to the early 1970s, electricity consumption grew at an annual rate of 7 percent—nearly twice as fast as total energy consumption—and the United States had to double its generating and transmission capacity every 10 years.

Electricity is generated by four principal fuels—coal, fuel oil, natural gas, and enriched uranium. Because domestic supplies of coal and uranium are relatively abundant, and because current and prospective prices for other fuels make coal and uranium relatively cheap, the Federal Energy Administration has encouraged the use of these two fuels in new generating plants.

In 1974, the electric-generating capacity of the United States was roughly 450 thousand megawatts. Because electricity rates soared with fuel costs after the embargo, and because of the national recession, electricity consumption remained fairly stable from 1973 through 1975. In 1974–75, therefore, utilities cancelled or deferred 141,000 megawatts of planned nuclear capacity additions and 75,000 megawatts of planned coal capacity additions.[38] Projected near-term generating capacity should be adequate for United States electricity demands through the late 1970s. However, given the lead time required for the expansion of baseload coal and nuclear generating capacity, the post-1973 decisions to defer new coal and nuclear power plants could give rise to shortages in the mid-1980s.[39]

Most utilities that cancel large nuclear or coal plants but still require additional capacity substitute jet turbine generators powered by either natural gas or distillate fuel oil. Jet turbines take only about two years to plan and install and entail an investment of about $200 per kilowatt hour of capacity. Planning and installation of new coal and nuclear baseload capacity take at least 8 and 10 years, respectively, and the investment requirements presently exceed $500 per kilowatt hour of capacity. Far lower fuel and amortization costs for coal and nuclear generating plants more than offset the lower capital costs of jet turbines. Nevertheless, because recently there has been enormous uncertainty about the future growth of electricity demand, levels of inflation and interest rates, and electricity rates, electric utilities have sought to delay making large investment decisions and to minimize their initial capital costs. Moreover, states that are often slow to approve rate hikes based on higher capital costs have readily allowed utilities to pass on higher fuel costs to consumers. Many electric utilities also have found that the easiest way to avoid environmental objections to the development of new coal and nuclear capacity is to rely on jet turbines. This substitution has been (and will continue to be) undesirable from both economic and national security perspectives. Besides costing consumers more, jet turbine electricity generation ultimately requires higher oil imports, making the United States more vulnerable than ever to future oil-import interruptions.

FUTURE ENERGY SUPPLIES

Assuming a $13 per barrel price for domestic crude oil (adjusted for inflation), the FEA estimates that, in 1985, aggregate United States energy production will total 83.8 quadrillion Btu (inferred from Table 3). This estimate is based on the assumption that United States energy production will grow at an average annual rate of nearly 4 percent between 1976 and 1985. But given the constraints on expanding production, a more plausible annual growth rate is probably between 3 and 3.5 percent. At this rate, total United States energy production will range between 78 quadrillion and 82 quadrillion Btu by 1985, and total energy independence (i.e., zero reliance on oil imports) will be possible only if annual demand growth averages less than 1 percent over the next nine years. If crude oil imports are allowed to stay at their 1975 levels (i.e., about 6 million barrels per day), total United States energy demands can grow at an average annual rate of 2.5 percent. Unfortunately, the United States economy seems likely to stagnate if the average annual growth in total energy demand is held to less than 2.5 percent. The prospect of either higher oil imports or inadequate energy supplies creates a policy dilemma.

FUTURE ENERGY DEMANDS

Just prior to the OAPEC embargo, total United States energy demands were growing at an annual rate slightly in excess of 4 percent. If, between 1976 and 1985, demand resumes growing at this rate, Americans will consume about 106 quadrillion Btu of energy in 1985, and oil imports will range between 11 and 13 million barrels per day.

Most Americans experienced substantial energy price hikes for the first time in 1973, following the start of the

OAPEC embargo. Quantitative estimates of the price-responsiveness of demand derived from preembargo data probably shed little light on postembargo energy consumption problems. (Quantitative estimates of the long-run price-elasticity of demand for most fuels range between −0.5 and −1.5.[40]) But as long as the real prices of all types of energy stay at their sharply higher postembargo levels, United States energy demands are unlikely to resume growing at their preembargo rate of 4 percent for any sustained time period.

Historically, this nation's energy demands have grown almost as fast as real GNP. The standard explanation for this historical constancy is that, because energy is a key input required to produce many of the goods and services comprising GNP, energy consumption must grow roughly as fast as real GNP. The chief flaw in this explanation is its failure to account for the effects of higher prices.

From the late 1800s to the 1973 OAPEC embargo, the relative price of energy consumed in the United States actually fell. Thus, most of the population chose to substitute increased energy inputs for other, relatively more expensive goods and productive factors, such as capital and labor. But if relative energy prices had instead risen, the number and extent of these substitutions would have been less. Evidence from inter-country comparisons suggests that some substantial demand reductions are possible in an economy that has a GNP similar to that of the United States but substantially higher energy prices.[41] For example, because of lower transportation costs, coking coal is much cheaper in the United States than in Japan, and the American steel industry consumes approximately 30 percent more coal than the Japanese steel industry per ton of steel produced. Likewise, largely because of excise tax differences, gasoline costs almost twice as much in Western Europe as in the United States. Western European countries also tax new, large cars more heavily than the United States. So it is not surprising that in the early 1970s, the typical European car got roughly twice as many miles per gallon as its American counterpart.

Policies to promote energy conservation may affect demand in the long run. Energy is used primarily to fuel or heat long-lived capital assets (e.g., steel plants, electricity generators, offices, and homes) and consumer durables (e.g., cars and appliances). Higher energy prices and incentives to promote conservation can prompt consumers to reduce home and office temperatures, drive less and more prudently, turn off lights, insulate homes, turn to more efficient appliances, and so on. Of course, consumers are not likely to voluntarily keep homes and offices at temperatures much below 68°F or ride a bicycle or use public transportation instead of driving, in response to either fuel price increases or government exhortations. Fewer still want their employers to cut back production and thus reduce employment in order to reduce fuel consumption. But in the long run, with the persistence of substantially higher fuel prices and/or policies that promote conservation, more acceptable energy-saving substitutions will become feasible as the existing stock of capital assets and consumer durables gradually depreciates and is replaced. Because of the long life of many capital assets and consumer durables, even if the United States adopts strong conservation measures, the transition to greater fuel economy in the various sectors of the economy may take 10 to 25 years.

Historically, United States real GNP has grown at a long-run average annual rate of about 3.5 percent. Because the United States is beginning to emerge from its worst postwar recession, most forecasts project the real GNP will grow at above-average rates (perhaps 5 to 6 percent) for the remainder of the 1970s. Most easy short-term energy-saving measures have already been implemented. Therefore, if the economy pulls out of recession, total United States energy demands may have to grow at an average annual rate of about 4 percent until 1980. By then, barring the unforeseen, many significant and permanent energy-saving substitutions will have been made. (The most important near-term fuel efficiency advances will probably be due to an automobile fleet that will become much more fuel-efficient as new cars replace old.) If the United States adopts strong measures to promote conservation, the rate of growth in United States energy demands may average as low as 2.5 percent in the 1980s, and total United States energy consumption will then total about 99 quadrillion Btu in

1985. If total 1985 domestic energy production is about 80 quadrillion Btu, the United States will be importing about 9 million barrels of oil per day in 1985 (compared with roughly 6.1 million barrels per day in 1975).

Assuming that foreign crude oil prices remain no lower than they were in early 1976 and that government policies encourage greater production of most domestic fuels (e.g., allow substantially higher prices for domestic crude oil and natural gas and impose no unexpected delays on the development of new petroleum sources in northern Alaska and the Outer Continental Shelf or new coal mines in the West), United States oil-import levels seem likely to rise sharply until the arrival of the first deliveries of Alaskan oil in late 1977. Oil imports should then remain fairly stable for the next eight years. In the absence of such policies, United States reliance on oil imports may rise to more than 12 million barrels per day in 1985.

3

Dealing with Energy Problems

PRICE CONTROLS

If the nation is to have an adequate supply of energy without a dangerously high level of oil imports, policymakers will have to adopt measures that will both reduce energy demands and stimulate exploration and development of new domestic supplies. Raising prices would serve both of these purposes, but crude oil and natural gas are currently subject to restrictive price controls. Milton Friedman observes:

> Economists may not know much. But we do know one thing very well: how to produce shortages and surpluses. Do you want to produce a shortage of any product? Simply have government fix and enforce a legal maximum price on the product which is less than the price that would otherwise prevail.[1]

The Natural Gas Act of 1938 authorized the Federal Power Commission to regulate interstate pipeline tariffs in order to "protect consumers against exploitation of the natural gas [pipeline] companies"[2] and to offset the "great economic power of the pipeline companies as compared with that of communities seeking natural gas."[3] All the communities in a given region obtained their natural gas from a single interstate pipeline, and the protection of consumers from a potential pipeline transportation monopoly was and remains a valid policy goal.

But the scope of the Natural Gas Act was ambiguous. Until the early 1950s, the FPC maintained that the act did not authorize regulation of the prices gas producers charged pipelines. No one opposed the FPC's ruling as long as natural gas wellhead prices remained near their Depression lows. But after World War II, natural gas demand increased sharply. Supplies gradually became tighter, and wellhead prices rose. Consumer representatives reacted to these higher prices by asking the FPC to reverse its decision on price controls, arguing that, as they saw it, natural gas producers were exercising monopoly power.[4] Consumer representatives argued also that higher natural gas prices do not lead to appreciably higher output but lead to windfall profits for owners and producers of natural gas.[5] In 1954, the Supreme Court ruled that the Natural Gas Act did require FPC regulation of wellhead prices.

The FPC adopted area-wide wellhead price ceilings in 1960. Thereafter, natural gas wellhead prices rose very slowly, even though demand continued to grow rapidly. The first victims of natural gas shortages were buyers of interruptible gas supplies; as the 1960s progressed, increasing numbers of these buyers had their gas supplies cut off in the midst of winter, when gas demands were at their highest. Interruptible natural gas supplies are sold to large industrial or institutional users at a lower price than that of noninterruptible supplies; the delivery of gas under such arrangements may be suspended at the seller's discretion. Since the late 1960s, in response to the worsening national gas shortage, producers have been forced to add two other rationing devices: blanket refusals to provide service for broad classes of potential consumers and curtailment of deliveries to customers with "firm" (i.e., noninterruptible) contracts.

From the close of World War II until the mid-1960s, natural gas was the fastest-growing major energy source in the United States. Its share of the energy consumed in the United States rose from one-eighth to one-third. However, United States natural gas production had virtually stopped growing in 1970, and production has been declining since 1972. The upshot has been an ever-worsening natural gas shortage that has spurred an undesirable growth in demand for natural gas' closest substitute, crude oil products. By 1975, the United States' average daily demand for natural gas exceeded supply by the equivalent of about 4 million barrels of crude oil. The coincidence of a steadily worsening natural gas shortage and a fall in United States crude oil production was the chief cause of the 30 percent annual growth in United States oil imports between 1970 and 1973.

Price controls on natural gas were always inefficient. Moreover, the savings that accrue to those fortunate consumers with access to natural gas at the artifically low ceiling price were always less than the sum of the revenues lost by natural gas suppliers and the higher energy costs borne by consumers denied gas service. Even more costly to the entire nation have been the increased reliance on foreign oil and—since natural gas is the cleanest-burning fossil fuel—increased environmental pollution.[6]

Price controls on crude oil and refined oil products are a more recent innovation. In 1973, the Cost of Living Council (CLC) set ceiling prices on all crude oil classified as old, that is, from leaseholds producing prior to 1973. The CLC believed the ceilings would help combat inflation and prevent owners and producers of already developed supplies from making windfall profits. In order to minimize the perverse incentives to reduce crude oil production, Congress explicitly exempted from price controls oil supplied by low-productivity (less than 10 barrels per day) stripper wells. Stripper oil production costs were already near the ceiling price and still rising because the costs of drilling equipment and supplies also were increasing. Price ceilings on stripper oil would have made it unprofitable to continue producing from marginal fields, to rework closed fields, and to boost output from stripper wells already in operation.

Recognizing that oil companies needed some incentive to expand exploration, development, and production from new sources, the CLC also exempted new crude oil—defined as production from leaseholds above the level achieved in 1973—from price ceilings. As an additional incentive to develop new oil, the council allowed producers to release a matching barrel of old oil from price ceilings for every barrel of new oil they produced. The exemptions granted to stripper, new, and released oil covered 35 to 40 percent of all domestic crude oil produced during 1974–75.

Before 1973, the price paid by oil refiners for any specified barrel of crude oil was determined by its economic value according to such criteria as potential gasoline content, level and kind of pollutants, and proximity to major refining and consuming centers. After 1973, the price of a barrel of crude oil depended also on whether it was classified as old, exempt, or foreign. Since late 1973, the average wellhead price of old oil has been fixed at $5.25 per barrel. But between October 1973 and January 1976, the average price of exempt domestic crude oil rose from about $6 to $13 per barrel—roughly the same as the delivered cost of imported oil.

Many months before the 1973–74 OAPEC oil embargo, it was evident that the price ceilings on old oil had been set far below market-clearing levels and that, as a result, shortages were developing. Crude-short refiners, desperate for refinery feedstocks, began bidding up the prices of exempt crude oil. They also sought ways to circumvent the price controls on old oil. Trade reports published before the OAPEC embargo indicate that one approach was to agree to "tie-in" sales. Specifically, both old and new oil would be purchased from a given supplier, but the buyer would pay the controlled price for old oil and a high enough price for new oil to bring the weighted average price for the total purchase almost to the market-clearing level. To prevent such tie-in purchases from totally emasculating the crude oil price controls, the Federal Energy Office (FEO) which had inherited the responsibility for administering crude oil price controls from the Cost of Living Council, froze all old oil buyer-seller arrangements as of December 1, 1973.

Some refiners processed higher proportions of cheap,

price-controlled old crude than did others. In order to keep these more fortunate refiners from accumulating windfall profits, the FEO enforced differential price ceilings on the prices charged for refined petroleum products; the maximum price each refiner could charge was determined by adding all cost increases to the price it charged during a preembargo base period. This pricing procedure resulted in intercompany price differences of as much as 12 cents per gallon for retail gasoline in the midst of the OAPEC embargo.

During the OAPEC embargo, all petroleum products were in such short supply that refiners who had high costs because they processed relatively small amounts of price-controlled old oil could charge higher prices for their products and not lose sales. But once the embargo ended and shortages eased, these high-cost companies would have had either to maintain higher prices and watch their sales plummet or to cut prices and suffer huge losses. To deal with this problem, the FEA introduced "entitlements." Specifically, refiners with above-industry-average old oil supplies have had to pay competitors with below-industry-average old oil supplies $6 to $8 per barrel for entitlements to refine their own old oil. In 1975, refiners with above-industry-average old oil supplies made entitlement payments totaling well over $1 billion to their competitors. If crude oil prices were not controlled, this cross-subsidization would be unnecessary.

The omnibus Energy Policy and Conservation Act of 1975 mandated a rollback in United States crude oil prices to a $7.66 per barrel weighted average on February 1, 1976.[7] Under this law, the President can raise domestic oil prices monthly (up to 10 percent per year), and all crude oil price controls are to expire after 40 months.

On January 7, 1976, the FEA issued proposals designed to comply with the new legislation's price control formula.[8] The FEA proposals called for maintaining the current $5.25 per barrel ceiling on old oil and placing an average $11.28 per barrel ceiling on new and stripper oil—a rollback of $1.18 per barrel from uncontrolled prices of September 1975. The FEA also recognized that, because an oil field's daily output naturally declines with production, the 1972 base used in the definition of old oil had become obsolete in many cases. The FEA therefore changed the base from an old leasehold's output in the corresponding month of 1972 to its average monthly production and sale of old crude during 1975.

Today, the FEA has roughly 1,400 employees who enforce the entitlement program as well as complex regulations aimed at ensuring fair prices for producers of different grades of oil.[9] The FEA has spent millions of dollars in promulgating and enforcing these price and allocation rules, and the oil companies have spent additional millions in trying to comply. In addition to requiring these administrative costs, the FEA pricing and allocation regulations have precipitated heated debates because each group of consumers and refiners has a different definition of "fair" allocation of low-cost petroleum. This politically charged atmosphere makes it difficult to draft and enact good energy policies.

Moreover, low prices for domestic oil subsidize higher levels of crude oil consumption while discouraging investments to expand domestic production. If below-market-clearing prices are temporary, the resulting supply-demand distortions do not necessarily lead to additional, costly domestic oil shortages. But oil prices have been controlled almost continuously since 1971, impeding United States efforts to reduce reliance on oil imports and increasing its vulnerability to further OPEC price hikes and renewed embargo threats. The FEA's recently released *National Energy Outlook* concludes that, if crude oil and natural gas prices are decontrolled and rise to levels equivalent to the present $13 per barrel delivered cost of imported oil, the United States will import about 5.9 million barrels of oil per day in 1985; if not, the United States will import 13.5 million barrels per day in 1985.[10]

If price controls were eliminated in late 1976, the average price of domestic crude oil would rise by about $5 per barrel to the $13 per barrel range; wellhead prices of most deregulated interstate natural gas would rise even more—from about 50 cents to about $2 per mcf. Price hikes of this magnitude raise the specter of oil companies, petroleum landowners, and others reaping windfall profits as a result of a sudden increase in economic rents. Those who favor continuation of crude oil and natural gas price controls presumably do so because they believe that the social benefits of reducing these windfall profits outweigh the large economic inefficiencies that controls create.[11] Unfortunately, both the public and energy policymakers often seem to be misinformed as to who actually benefits from higher energy prices and how much they benefit. As a result, policy debates have too frequently centered on reducing alleged oil company windfalls rather than on achieving other, possibly more important, energy policy goals.

During the 10 years prior to the OAPEC embargo, the profits of most United States oil companies were below the average for all United States industries according to the most common measure, the rate of return on equity investment. Largely as a result of embargo-related shortages and higher oil prices, profits of 28 of the largest oil companies rose 53 percent in 1973 and an additional 41 percent in 1974. In 1974, the rate of return on equity reached 17.4 percent (the figure for all United States manufacturing was roughly 14.5 percent), but in 1975, it went down to roughly 12 percent.

Geological variation in the size and productivity of oil and gas fields causes enormous variations in total unit production costs. For example, northern Alaska's giant Prudhoe Bay oil field has proven reserves of 9.6 billion barrels, and the typical well is expected initially to produce 10,000-plus barrels per day; total production costs (exclusive of all taxes, royalties, and lease bonuses) for this oil should be less than $2 per barrel at the wellhead. In many other parts of the United States, however, individual crude oil wells produce only one or two barrels daily, and the production costs for this oil frequently exceed $10 per barrel.

Every petroleum producer would like to produce from the very-lowest-cost sources. Most oil producers cannot do so because the supply known to be available from such sources is insufficient to meet current demand. To satisfy demand, producers must use higher-cost sources as well. But they will produce from these sources only if the price of oil is high enough to cover their total costs. When the price of oil reaches that level, the owners of oil from lower-cost sources will reap "rents"—payments in excess of total production costs (which include a competitive return to stockholders). For example, because the United States does not have sufficient domestic oil reserves to satisfy present demands, it imports oil at a cost of about $13 per barrel. Therefore, in the absence of crude oil price controls, those who own domestic oil costing less than $13 per barrel to produce and transport to American refineries reap substantial rents.

Postembargo price hikes for foreign oil led directly to substantial windfall profits (that is, higher rents, because revenues rose far more rapidly than costs) for both the oil-exporting countries and all owners of domestic oil or oil substitutes not subject to price controls. But the companies that produce crude oil have not been the biggest beneficiaries of these windfall profits. Oil producers must purchase production rights and pay royalties and production taxes before they can produce oil from any specified land parcel, and these fees and taxes rise whenever the price of oil rises; hence, the biggest beneficiaries of these oil windfalls have been those who own or can tax oil lands.

The OPEC countries have been far and away the largest beneficiaries of the higher energy prices paid by Americans since 1973. The United States now imports more than 40 percent of its total oil needs. In addition to paying all production and transportation costs, the companies that sell this oil also pay to the exporting countries taxes and royalties that typically exceed $11 per barrel.

The owners and taxers of domestic petroleum lands have also received large windfalls. Besides paying all production costs (which are typically much higher in the United States than in the OPEC countries), companies that produce domestic crude oil must pay lease bonuses to the landowner in return for exclusive production rights to all crude oil or natural gas, royalties (traditionally set at either 12.5 or 16.67 percent of the petroleum's wellhead value) to the landowner when any petroleum is produced, and severance taxes up to 5 percent of the petroleum's wellhead value to the state in which the petroleum is located in return for the privilege of "severing" the petroleum from the land. Whenever petroleum prices rise, lease bonuses, royalties, and severance taxes tend to follow suit. Because the two largest owners of domestic petroleum lands are the federal government and the largest oil-producing states, they, not the oil companies, are the largest recipients of the higher royalties and lease bonuses attributable to an oil price rise. In addition, these governments receive higher revenues from severance taxes. Of course, those private citizens and companies who own oil lands have also benefited from the oil price rise. But federal and state governments also collect a substantial fraction of these windfalls through their taxation of personal and corporate income.

The chief purpose of price controls on domestic crude oil and natural gas has been to reduce the size of the windfalls received by their producers. But enforcement of these controls also subsidizes those consumers fortunate enough to be able to purchase these fuels at the low market-controlled prices. It is not obvious that this class of consumers is more deserving than those who are unable to buy the price-controlled product.

Underlying all arguments for price controls is concern for the hardships that decontrolled prices would impose on consumers. The conventional wisdom has it that high energy prices have a differentially adverse impact on consumers with low incomes because direct consumption of energy does not rise in proportion to income. But an MIT study group has recently questioned this assumption:

> Families with incomes below the median spend about 11 percent of their income on gasoline, electricity, heat, and other forms of energy. The fraction declines with rising income—families with incomes of $12,000 spend a little less than 8 percent on energy, and those with incomes of $20,000 around 5 percent. It appears to us, however, that the FEA substantially overstates the distributional effects of an increase in energy prices. The Ford Foundation's Energy Policy Project studied the issue more carefully using a survey of energy consumption made recently. They confirm the FEA's finding that direct consumption

of energy does not rise in proportion to income. However, the EPP study shows that consumption of energy through purchase of goods that are produced with energy is twice as important as direct consumption, and does rise more nearly in proportion. Further, both the FEA and EPP studies suffer from an important technical defect that biases them toward understating them in high income groups. The lower income groups contain many families who are normally better off but have suffered a temporary reduction in income. These families consume more than do the genuinely poor. Similarly, the upper income groups contain families who are only temporarily well off and cannot consume as much as the genuinely rich. An important next step in research should be the adjustment for this bias by methods of budget analysis that are currently available. *It is not at all unlikely that a refined study would reveal that total energy consumption is the same fraction of income in all groups, and that an increase in energy prices does not have an adverse effect on the distribution of income.*[12]

The MIT study group's analysis does not directly address the issue of poverty. It merely raises questions about the evidence that the poor spend proportionately more of their income on energy (see Tables 6 and 7). If this proposition is not

Table 6   Percentage of Family Income Spent on Energy

INCOME STATUS	AVERAGE HOUSEHOLD INCOME	AVERAGE ANNUAL BTU (MILLION PER HOUSEHOLD)	AVERAGE ANNUAL COST PER HOUSEHOLD	PERCENT- AGE OF TOTAL INCOME SPENT ON ENERGY
Poor	$ 2,500	207	$379	15.2
Lower middle	8,000	294	572	7.2
Upper middle	14,000	403	832	5.9
Well off	24,500	478	994	4.1

Source: Energy Policy Project of the Ford Foundation, *A Time to Choose*, p. 118.

Table 7   Annual Indirect Use of Energy

INCOME STATUS	AVERAGE HOUSEHOLD INCOME	TOTAL INDIRECT HOUSEHOLD ENERGY CONSUMPTION (MILLION BTU)
Poor	$ 2,500	353
Lower middle	8,000	549
Upper middle	14,000	843
Well off	24,500	1,095

Source: Energy Policy Project of the Ford Foundation, *A Time to Choose*, p. 126.

valid, then higher energy prices do not necessarily have a regressive effect on income distribution, although a poor person who has to spend more for energy may still suffer more than one who is richer. If the nation seeks to help the poor, direct assistance may be more efficient and equitable than energy subsidies.

United States policymakers must decide whether the large inefficiencies and inequities caused by continued enforcement of oil and gas price controls are outweighed by the windfalls that would result from their elimination. In an attempt to reduce this efficiency-equity conflict, a variety of alternatives to total decontrol have been proposed:

1. Decontrolling only the prices of high-cost and/or newly discovered and developed reserves of crude oil and natural gas

2. Decontrolling prices but taxing windfall profits

3. Decontrolling prices but requiring reinvestment of all additional profits in exploration and development for domestic petroleum

4. Decontrolling prices and levying an excise tax on domestic fuels

5. Allowing the price of domestic fuels to rise as high as but no higher than the "long-run supply price"—the price at which the government feels the nation will not be excessively reliant on oil imports

These proposals raise a variety of questions. For example, how should the government define and measure windfall profits? How should it define new oil or natural gas? At what level should the excise tax be set in order not to discourage additional domestic exploration and development? What is the long-run supply price? Compared with these administratively complicated quasi-decontrol formulas, total decontrol has the virtues of simplicity and economic efficiency.

ENERGY CONSERVATION

Americans are the world's largest energy consumers. The United States has about 5 percent of the world's population but consumes approximately 30 percent of its energy. Long before the OAPEC embargo, many critics of United States energy policy advocated energy conservation measures. Since the embargo, United States policymakers have tried to accelerate public acceptance of energy conservation. They have contemplated both mandatory fuel-efficiency standards and economic incentives—such as higher fuel prices or subsidies—to promote conservation.

As a conservation measure, the Energy Policy and Conservation Act of 1975 has inconsistencies. On the one hand, it requires manufacturers of consumer durables that use significant amounts of energy (e.g., automobiles, water heaters, air conditioners, furnaces, and television sets) to comply with new energy-efficiency labeling requirements and to begin taking steps to make products that consume appreciably less energy.[13] The fuel-efficiency standards for new automobiles are especially strict—mileage must rise from a present average of about 18 miles per gallon to an average of 27.5 per gallon in 1985. This act also sets targets for "maximum improvements" in energy efficiency by firms engaged in the 10 most energy-consumptive industries. On the other hand, the act also rolls back crude oil prices by an average of $1.18 per barrel. Lower prices can only encourage greater and less efficient energy use.

Setting and enforcing explicit, well-defined energy consumption standards is probably the cheapest and quickest method of reducing fuel consumption when a good commercial technology for conforming to the standard is already well established and can be readily implemented at an acceptable cost over the time period allotted.

But in some cases, no good, commercial energy-saving technology is available. In such cases, the costs of enforcing mandatory standards may outweigh the conservation benefits. In addition, the need to satisfy stringent near-term standards may force companies to make expensive modifications of the existing technology rather than to do the time-consuming research and development necessary to introduce a substantially different, but ultimately better, commercial technology.

For example, it is an enormous job to modify an automobile assembly line substantially and quickly. But the federal clean air and safety standards adopted in 1970 required automobile manufacturers to make such modifications by 1973. The effort to meet these standards in such a short period raised the cost of producing the average car by $300 to $500 and resulted in a substantial deterioration in motor vehicle fuel efficiency. By 1974, some of these standards (e.g., the seat belt interlock system) had been judged so unreasonable or costly that they were either abolished or delayed. Automobile manufacturers ultimately developed a new commercial technology—the catalytic converter—that reduced air emissions and increased fuel efficiency. But on balance, hindsight suggests that the 1970 clean air and safety standards tried to accomplish too much in too short a time. (Similar objections have been levied against many other types of pollution standards.)

The Energy Policy and Conservation Act of 1975 gives automobile manufacturers 10 years in which to meet fuel-efficiency standards. It also promises consumers sizable benefits in the form of lower fuel costs. Hence, both producers and consumers seem likely to find the new motor vehicle fuel-efficiency standards easier and less costly to meet than the post-1969 air emission and safety standards. But cars manufactured in compliance with the strict 1985 standards will be much smaller and lighter than current models, posing increased safety risks and reducing consumer choice. Today at least, many Americans choose to pay higher fuel costs in return for greater motor vehicle size and safety. The stringent automobile fuel-efficiency standards imposed by the 1975 act effectively abolish this option.

The Ford Foundation's Energy Policy Project observes: "Consumer or final demand for energy is influenced by price, consumer preferences, and income. Relative price—the price of energy in relation to prices for other goods—is especially important."[14] Higher fuel prices encourage consumers to make less use of energy-intensive products and to use these products more prudently; provide a strong incentive to manufacturers to develop more energy-efficient products, which can be priced higher than competitors' less efficient products; and facilitate the allocation of scarce resources to their most valuable uses as judged by the market test.

Taxes are an appropriate policy tool if the government wishes to raise energy prices in order to promote greater conservation; the government, not the seller, receives the additional revenues and, presumably, can either raise public spending or grant offsetting cuts in other taxes. The United States government has often placed high excise taxes on luxury or socially undesirable products, such as liquor and tobacco, to raise revenues and to discourage, but not prohibit, their consumption. Many observers have suggested that large, high-gasoline-consuming cars equipped with air conditioners and high-horsepower engines offer an appropriate target for energy-conserving luxury taxes. In addition, an annual excise tax that could be collected when the owner pays his state registration fee might encourage quicker scrapping of cars that consume above-average amounts of gasoline.

Another type of conservation tax that has been widely discussed is a high (and, over time, rising) excise tax on gasoline. The federal government might levy a gasoline excise tax that would rise annually by 10 cents per gallon to a maximum of $1 per gallon. Several Western European countries now have even higher gasoline taxes. Most proponents of a high gasoline excise tax recommend offsetting cuts in other federal taxes to prevent either an undesirable reduction in aggregate demand—and thus a rise in unemployment—or undesirable increases in the living costs of most Americans.

The government also might promote energy conservation by subsidizing the purchase of energy-conserving consumer durables or capital investments through such measures as tax credits to homeowners who install additional insulation or to firms that make fuel-saving investments.

DEVELOPING HIGH-COST ENERGY ALTERNATIVES

The United States has enough coal reserves to support continued substantial economic growth well past 1990. But unless discoveries of new crude oil and natural gas reserves in the Outer Continental Shelf and northern Alaska prove far larger than any authorities presently anticipate, United States production of both fuels will resume declining before 1990. If the United States is to continue to expand its total energy production thereafter, it will have to create new technologies and provide adequate economic incentives for a dramatic expansion of our presently economical crude oil reserves, the commercial production of synthetic fuels from either coal or oil shale, and much greater use of coal and nuclear power in the form of electricity. Large-scale commercial development of these sources will take more than 10 years and cost billions of dollars. At present crude oil and natural gas prices and with the known technology, the production of most of these fuels is uneconomic without large subsidies.

Even greater investments and more time are necessary to establish the feasibility of commercial production of energy using breeder reactors, geothermal power, biomass power, tidal power, wind power, wave power, solar power, and fusion. Geothermal, tidal, and solar power have been used in localized, relatively small-scale applications, but their feasibility for large-scale use remains to be demonstrated. Moreover, even if the production of energy from these exotic alternative energy sources proves feasible, it might still pose insurmountable economic or environmental problems.

Because of these uncertainties, and because even success-ful efforts are likely to involve extremely long lead times and huge expenditures, private companies have been unwilling and unable to sponsor the basic research and development programs that are required if some of these energy sources are to become commercial within the next several decades as the United States' and the world's production of oil and gas from presently conventional petroleum sources begins its projected decline.

A case can be made for having the government offer assurances that (1) the basic research necessary to establish the technical as well as theoretical feasibility of producing energy from presently exotic, but potentially competitive, sources is undertaken on an appropriate scale and (2) the huge de-velopment expenditures that will be necessary to demonstrate the feasibility of large-scale production are made. Assuming that the technical and environmental feasibility of large-scale production can be demonstrated, private investors can then be relied upon to produce commercial quantities of energy from those sources that appear likely to be competitive with conven-tional fuels.

Those advocating federal support of the basic research and initial (precommercial) development necessary to dem-onstrate the feasibility of producing large quantities of energy from presently noncommercial sources must answer two questions: How large a resource commitment should the government make when subsidizing the production of pres-ently noncommercial domestic energy sources? And what is the most efficient way to spend those public resources au-thorized for subsidizing energy?

In 1975, President Ford offered at least a partial answer to both questions when he proposed the $100 billion Energy Independence Authority (EIA) to encourage large-scale pro-duction of energy from a variety of sources that currently are noncompetitive with either conventional fossil fuels or nuclear power.[15]

There is a high probability that the EIA bill either will not be passed or will be passed only in considerably altered form. Nevertheless, as a prelude to consideration of possible meth-

ods for encouraging faster development of currently uneconomic alternative fuels, it is instructive to examine the way in
which EIA's proponents seek, by subsidizing investments in
projects that would not be financed otherwise, to achieve the
goal of substantially increasing the United States' domestic
energy supplies in an environmentally safe manner. The assumption underlying the EIA is that, although over the next
decade most new energy projects will continue to be financed
entirely by private investors, certain desirable projects—high-
cost and/or high-risk because they rely on as yet commercially
unproven technologies or must be undertaken on a very large
scale—require substantial subsidies if they are to produce com-
merical quantities of energy. Most notable among these
projects are synthetic production (coal gasification and lique-
faction and oil production from shale), uranium enrichment
and other aspects of nuclear power generation, and development of a few conventional fossil fuel power sources now
hampered by unusually high production costs (e.g., some electricity generation and extraction of low-grade heavy crude oils
or of natural gas in "tight," nonpermeable formations). If the
EIA bill is passed, the President's advisers project that alternative sources can supply the energy equivalent of 10 to 15
million barrels per day of new crude oil by 1985. They estimate
that the total investment necessary to achieve this level of
additional production is $600 billion (in 1975 dollars), and EIA
would be authorized to supply $100 billion of this total—
raising $25 billion by selling equity to the U.S. Treasury and
issuing federally guaranteed debt to raise an additional $75
billion. The remaining $500 billion would be supplied by pri-
vate firms.

Firms would submit project proposals and subsidy re-
quests to the EIA. Although the EIA would not make direct
grants-in-aid, it would be authorized to grant "any form of
advance, extension of credit, investment participation or
guarantee, including, without limitation, loans, guarantee of
obligations, guarantees of price, purchase and leaseback of
facilities, and the purchase of convertible or equity securi-
ties."[16] The proposed legislation also contains an ambiguous
provision to the effect that, if a project generates profits as a

result of the EIA's financial aid, the EIA will share these profits in proportion to the financial risk assumed. Total aid to any firm would be limited to no more than 10 percent of the EIA's capital and should "not enhance the recipients' competitive positions."[17] The legislation would prevent the EIA from becoming a permanent federal presence in the energy industry by restricting its acquisition of a controlling or operating interest in any energy project to a temporary, "turnkey" arrangement running no more than two years. Moreover, the EIA would not be allowed to make new aid commitments after June 30, 1983, and would terminate all operations and liquidate all holdings and obligations by June 30, 1986.

Discussion of the EIA bill has been postponed indefinitely in committee, and a less expensive but similar proposal to encourage commercial development of coal synthetics has been defeated in Congress. Opposition to the EIA bill centers both on its high cost and its cumbersome financing provisions and on fears that it will unduly subsidize large energy producers. But a more telling criticism appears to be that this bill fails to take proper account of the limited state of present basic knowledge about most of the alternative fuels.

An MIT study group recently gave its assessment of the near-term potential of alternative energies:

> Shale oil and [coal] gasification are the most advanced of the new technologies. Uncertainties for less advanced technologies, such as geothermal and solar energy, are even larger. In light of these costs and uncertainties, pre-1985 commercial development of a synthetic fuels industry or of other technologies is unlikely. . . . However, because of the long lead time involved in both research and development, decisions made today will determine the future options available. . . . In the first instance, which technologies offer promise? These priorities must be established in order to develop a coherent research and development policy.[18]

Assuming that the MIT analysis is even roughly correct, a program of the size and scope of the EIA must be judged unrealistically large in the 1975–85 time frame. Given the absence of detailed knowledge about the necessary commercial technology, a program designed to encourage large-scale, near-term commercial production of alternative fuels will raise the nation's energy costs unnecessarily. In addition, such a program would place enormous new demands on the environment. At this time a smaller but still substantial program to develop the necessary basic technology and demonstrate the feasibility of producing large quantities of energy from sources that are not commercial at present is probably more cost-effective.

In cases in which the basic technology for producing unconventional energy is thought to be nearly in hand and in which environmental problems are judged surmountable, a less ambitious institution might be preferable to the EIA. Specifically, a relatively small energy authority could be empowered to (1) decide which general types of alternative energy projects show the most promise of becoming commercial by 1985 (after discussion with government and private technical experts); (2) specify what energy projects are most promising and what standards each of these projects is required to meet; and (3) solicit competitive bids from all companies wishing to own and manage these projects—subject to their satisfying minimum financial, environmental, technical, and product-quality standards and assuming that they agree to share with other interested parties any technical knowledge derived from these projects. The company that requested the lowest minimum price guarantee for a specified output of the alternative fuel would be declared the winner of the bidding competition.

Compared with the EIA, this method of subsidizing commercial production of high-cost but technically feasible alternative energies has three advantages. First, in order to be considered, all proposals for a specific project would have to satisfy the minimum financial, technical, environmental, and product-quality standards; the winning bid would be the one that best satisfied one criterion—the minimum price guarantee per barrel of crude oil equivalents. This approach would simplify the job of choosing among alternatives and reduce opportunities for abuse. Second, the vigorous competition among all firms trying to win a specific project subsidy would tend to limit the subsidy. Third, the subsidy provides an incentive to develop and install cost-cutting processes. Because the proposed energy authority would require that knowledge of all subsidized processes be shared freely, the entire nation would ultimately gain.

Guaranteeing a minimum price is an inappropriate form of subsidy for those fuels for which no promising commercial technology is available or which present serious environmental problems. In these instances, the solicitation of competitive bids for the lowest minimum price guarantee for a specified output of fuel is unlikely to attract any bids from private investors. When the government decides to subsidize this type of high-risk project, it should probably consider two quite different methods: either direct government ownership and management of the project (perhaps using an organization modeled after the Tennessee Valley Authority) or government grants to private companies which would be convertible into loans if the project proved successful. The first method has the virtues of potentially eliminating the possibility of excessive subsidies to private firms and improving coordination among government agencies. The second method has the virtue of reducing private investors' front-end costs and risks without providing unnecessary subsidies for projects that prove commercially acceptable. In choosing between these two strategies, it is important to assess whether the managers of a government-owned energy company can achieve sufficient independence and leeway. Can they function properly if they must also consider the political ramifications of their day-to-day operation? Can they be insulated from direct political interference by other government officials who are not aware of the constraints on what should be basically business decisions or who oppose specific decisions? Failure to address these questions is likely to create severe administrative problems in a business that, by definition, is very risky and requires high levels of technical expertise.

OIL-MONOPOLY PROBLEMS[19]

Between 1969 and 1976, the cost of a barrel of average-quality foreign crude oil delivered to the United States' East Coast rose from about $2.30 to about $13. As a result, prices for all domestic crude oil products and their substitutes—chiefly coal, natural gas, and uranium—also soared. Public consternation at these price increases prompted a variety of widely quoted public opinion makers, both in and out of government, to charge that many United States energy problems could be traced to the monopolistic abuses of the giant, politically powerful integrated oil companies.

Large, vertically integrated oil companies are involved in many phases of the energy business. They produce and sell domestic as well as foreign crude oil, transport crude oil from wellhead to refinery, ship refined products to marketers, and sell a variety of refined products and petrochemicals directly, at wholesale or retail levels. They are also significant suppliers of other kinds of energy, including natural gas, coal, and uranium ores. Three types of evidence shed light on whether these companies have monopolized or are able to monopolize one or more of the energy markets:

1. *Market structure:* The most competitive markets generally contain many strong companies and can be easily entered by new firms or by firms doing business in other, often related, industries.

2. *Firm conduct:* Agreements to fix prices, divide markets, or use legal and marketing tactics that tend to harass present or potential competitors are common forms of explicitly anticompetitive market conduct. Sometimes, companies that sell products in markets with relatively few firms behave in parallel fashion, although they do not formally collude. Because of conflicting pricing goals and insoluble planning problems, such implicit collusion is almost never found in industries with many

firms facing dissimilar and uncertain costs and demands.

3. *Profit rate:* Persistent and otherwise inexplicably high profits may result from monopolistic practices.

Judged by these three criteria, the countries belonging to OPEC currently exercise enormous monopoly power. The OPEC nations, which account for more than 95 percent of the non-Communist international crude oil trade, meet regularly to fix international oil prices. They have little to fear from new entrants into the market because most of the world's known low-cost oil supplies are within their borders and because no new, large non-OPEC sources can be found and developed until at least the 1980s. Finally, the $11 to $12 per barrel price that the OPEC countries charged for nearly all the crude oil they sold in 1976 is 10 to 100 times greater than their total unit production costs.

Tables 8 to 11 summarize market-share data for the largest firms participating in each stage of the domestic oil business. According to these data, the eight largest firms do not account for more than 64 percent of the total market at any stage and the largest firm never accounts for as much as 10 percent of the total. Judged by market share, the American oil industry is far less concentrated than most other American manufacturing or mining industries containing one or more giant firms (e.g., aluminum, automobiles, electrical equipment, and steel).

Many economists feel that the ease with which new firms can enter an industry offers better evidence of competition than do market-share data. Professor James McKie has described the ways firms enter the crude oil business:

Many oil-producing companies originated as successful wildcat enterprises. While a few firms may begin with a large supply of capital and immediately undertake an extensive drilling program, the typical firm got its start through a series of fortunate single ventures, often involving exploratory deals with established major or independent firms. New corporations and partnerships are fre-

Table 8 Company Shares of Domestic Net Crude Oil Production and Proven Domestic Crude Oil Reserves

COMPANY	SHARE OF DOMESTIC PRODUCTION (IN 1969), %	SHARE OF DOMESTIC PROVEN RESERVES (IN 1970), %
Exxon U.S.A.	9.76	9.92
Texaco	8.47	9.31
Gulf	6.78	8.97
Shell	6.08	5.98
SOCAL	5.31	8.97
ARCO	5.11	7.48
Standard of Indiana	5.09	8.46
Mobil	3.94	4.87
Getty	3.38	3.85
Union	2.88	3.18
Sun	2.47	2.67
Continental	2.21	2.77
Marathon	1.64	2.37
Phillips	1.55	3.55
Cities Service	1.28	2.49
Amerada Hess	1.04	2.49
Tenneco	0.99	0.90
Skelly	0.88	1.09
Superior	0.74	1.03
Top 4	31.09	34.18
Top 8	50.54	63.96

Source: Federal Trade Commission, *Preliminary Federal Trade Commission Staff Report on Its Investigation of the Petroleum Industry,* 1973, Tables II-1 and II-2.

quently budded from the existing ones. . . . A geologist or petroleum engineer may gain enough experience on his own, making good use of associations he has built up in the industry. . . . An employee of a drilling contractor may work up from platform hand to superintendent. Once known to purchasers of drilling services and sellers of equipment, he finds it relatively easy to set up his own firm. . . . After operating as a contract driller for some time, he may be willing to put one of his rigs into a wildcat venture on a speculative basis. . . . In this way drilling contractors frequently become independent producers. . . .

Table 9   Top 20 Companies' Share of U.S. Gasoline Refining Capacity, 1970

COMPANY	SHARE, %	CUMULATIVE SHARES
Exxon U.S.A.	9.22	9.22
Texaco	9.19	18.41
Indiana Standard	7.94	26.35
Shell	7.69	34.04
SOCAL	6.72	40.76
Gulf	6.47	47.23
Mobil	6.30	53.53
ARCO	6.25	59.78
Sun	4.54	64.32
Phillips	4.24	68.56
Union	3.24	71.80
SOHIO	3.09	74.89
Cities Service	2.26	77.15
Ashland	2.11	79.26
Continental	2.03	81.29
Marathon	1.92	83.21
Getty	1.76	84.97
Tenneco	1.35	86.32
Clark	1.21	87.53
American Petrofina	0.85	88.38

Source: Federal Trade Commission, *Preliminary Federal Trade Commission Staff Report on Its Investigation of the Petroleum Industry*, 1973, Table II-3.

Another way to enter oil and gas exploration is via brokerage. Exploration enterprise swarms with middlemen anxious to arrange producing deals. . . . A speculative broker may arrange a prospecting deal among other parties . . . and usually retains for himself a small interest in the venture. Since technical training and apprenticeship are not strictly necessary, this route is crowded with hopeful shoestring promoters along with the experienced entrepreneurs.[20]

Professor M. A. Adelman has written about the world tanker market:

Each individual ship available for spot charter is, in effect, like a separate firm and the worldwide market allows no

Table 10   Share of U.S. Gasoline Market, 1973

COMPANY	PERCENTAGE OF U.S. MARKET	CUMULATIVE SHARES
Texaco	7.97	7.97
Exxon	7.64	15.61
Shell	7.47	23.08
Indiana Standard	6.90	29.98
Gulf	6.75	36.73
Mobil	6.49	43.22
SOCAL	4.78	48.00
ARCO	4.37	52.37
Phillips	3.92	56.29
Sun	3.67	59.96
Union	3.05	63.01
Continental	2.30	65.31
Cities Service	1.66	66.97
Marathon	1.52	68.49
Ashland	1.48	69.97
Clark	1.25	71.22
SOHIO	1.23	72.45
Hess	1.00	73.45
BP	0.81	74.26
Tenneco	0.78	75.04
Murphy	0.66	75.70
Getty	0.65	76.35
American Petrofina	0.63	76.98
Skelly	0.60	77.58
Triangle	0.57	78.15

Source: Harold Wilson, "Exxon and Shell Score Gasoline Gains," *Oil and Gas Journal,* June 3, 1974, p. 78. Cites results of the Lundberg survey.

protected enclaves. . . . In any given month, several dozen ships are offered for oil company use all over the world by several hundred owners, none with over 5 percent of total tonnage. Tacit collusion would be impossible, and no attempt at open collusion has been made since World War II. . . . [The] "spot" charter market therefore seems purely competitive.

The time-charter market is linked to the spot market at one end, and at the other to the cost of creating new capacity. Here entry is open and cheap. . . . Moreover, there are no strong economies of scale in ship operations.

Table 11   Concentration in Petroleum-Product Markets

PERCENTAGE OF TOTAL UNITED STATES
REFINED PRODUCT SALES

	1976	1970	1974
Four largest firms	34.8	33.8	31.2
Eight largest firms	61.7	57.0	52.3

PERCENTAGE OF TOTAL UNITED STATES GASOLINE SALES

	1970	1974
Four largest firms	30.8	29.9
Eight largest firms	55.0	51.9

INDEPENDENTS' SHARE OF REFINED PRODUCTS

	1968	1974
Marketing	19.8	29.0
Refining	26.8	29.8

Source: Presentation by Ted Eck, Standard Oil of Indiana, reprinted in Bureau of National Affairs, *Energy Users' Report,* November 13, 1975, p. A-19.

Many owners have only one ship. . . . But to say that many competent firms cluster on the boundaries of the industry, and that minimum capital requirements are low, is to say that entry is easy and market control impossible.

With many ships available in the short-run, and easy entry for the long-run, what possibility is left for control in the meantime? Little if any in theory, and none can be observed in practice. Tankship owners, oil companies and independents cannot control the long-term supply even in concert, for anyone contemplating a production or refining investment and needing the transport services has time to charter a ship or buy a new one.[21]

And Professor Leonard Weiss has testified as an expert witness for the Justice Department's Antitrust Division in *U.S. v. I.B.M.* about entry into petroleum refining:

I mentioned . . . the number of firms, including some independents I have never heard of, who set out to build refineries between May and July of 1973 [immediately after oil import quotas were abolished], and it is just astounding—and these were one hundred million dollars and many one hundred million dollar investments—that shook my belief in capital requirements as a high barrier to entry quite a bit.[22]

Some oil industry critics assert that the participation of the major oil firms in joint ventures (usually confined to crude oil and pipelines) makes the usual measures of market concentration meaningless. Few empirical studies of joint ventures have been undertaken. But a recent empirical study by Professors Edward Erickson and Robert Spann concludes that:

> When structure is considered alone, the U.S. petroleum industry is one of the least concentrated of U.S. industries. . . . [However,] the firms in the petroleum industry engage in a number of joint activities, including joint ventures to bid for and develop offshore OCS leases. We have examined the record of the sealed bid auction market for offshore OCS lease sales from 1954 through mid-1973. We compared the patterns of bidding behavior and the composition of joint ventures with those which can reasonably be expected to have prevailed were the practice of forming joint ventures for offshore lease sales an example of collusive or anti-competitive behavior. The implications of such behavior are that joint ventures would be substituted for solo bids, that joint ventures would lead to stable market shares of OCS tracts won, that the incidence of joint ventures would be positively correlated with firm size, that majors and non-majors would not enter joint ventures together, and that identical bids might be observed.
>
> The facts are uniformly inconsistent with these implications. As the risks and uncertainties associated with offshore exploration became more widely understood, an increased incidence of joint ventures was associated with an increase in the total number of bidders, an increased number of bidders per tract, and a decrease in the relative number of tracts which receive only one bid. For smaller firms, by decreasing the variance associated with expending a given exploration budget, joint ventures decrease the chance of gambler's ruin in offshore exploration.

Majors have been much more likely to enter joint ventures which contained no other majors rather than joint ventures which contain two or more majors. . . .

Joint ventures, including joint ventures among major and non-major firms, have facilitated entry into offshore activity and have increased the number of bidders. In terms of their effect upon competitive results, joint ventures in offshore OCS lease auctions are pro-competitive.[23]

Most large oil companies are also significant suppliers of natural gas; many are substantial participants in the coal industry; and some are making preparations to enter the uranium enrichment business. Are these products sold in monopolistic markets? Has the participation of oil companies in coal and natural gas markets had an anticompetitive effect? Because crude oil and natural gas are frequently found in the same places and utilize the same production technology, real economies are available to firms that can produce both products, and large crude oil producers have almost inevitably become large producers of natural gas.

One of the principal justifications for natural gas wellhead price controls was that without price regulation, natural gas producers would be able to exercise substantial monopoly power. But the market-share data presented in Table 12 suggest that the natural gas industry is not highly concentrated. And numerous detailed studies by Professor Paul MacAvoy and his colleagues[24] buttress MacAvoy's conclusion that: "Studies of most field and supply markets in Texas, Louisiana, Oklahoma, etc. indicate the presence of systematic competition or monopsony throughout the period in which regulation was proposed. The problem to be solved by regulation seems not to have existed."[25]

More than 3,500 companies produce coal in the United States. Table 13 lists the 20 largest coal producers in 1972. Together, these 20 firms accounted for only 55 percent of total domestic production. Some of these firms are known chiefly for their interests in other industries. For example, Peabody Coal, the industry's largest producer, is presently owned by

Table 12 Company Shares of Natural Gas Sold to Interstate Pipelines, 1970

RANK	PRODUCER	VOLUME, MCF	PERCENT- AGE OF TOTAL	CUMULATIVE PERCENTAGE
1	Exxon	1,300,642,683	9.0	9.0
2	Gulf Oil	813,738,549	5.6	14.6
3	Shell Oil	785,667,041	5.4	20.0
4	Pan American Petroleum (Standard of Indiana)	767,430,589	5.3	25.3
5	Phillips	707,235,036	4.9	30.2
6	Mobil Oil	650,890,489	4.5	34.7
7	Texaco	607,433,789	4.2	38.9
8	Atlantic-Richfield	561,540,880	3.9	42.8
9	Union Oil of California	548,896,648	3.8	46.6
10	Continental Oil	461,297,727	3.2	49.8
11	California Co. Division of Chevron	367,213,888	2.5	52.3
12	Sun Oil	361,622,934	2.5	54.8
13	Alberta & Southern Gas (Canadian)	304,529,422	2.1	56.9
14	Tenneco	252,971,722	1.8	58.7
15	Cities Service	243,511,899	1.7	60.4
16	Superior Oil	240,211,285	1.7	62.1
17	Westcoast Transmission (Canadian)	223,257,230	1.5	63.6
18	Trans-Canada P.L.Ltd.	199,655,647	1.4	65.0
19	Pennzoil Producing	184,440,676	1.3	66.3
20	Getty Oil	173,480,911	1.2	67.5
	Total: Top 20	9,502,706,323		
	Total: Other	4,938,030,621		
	Grand total	14,440,736,944		

Source: Federal Power Commission, *Sales by Producers of Natural Gas to Interstate Pipeline Companies, 1970,* cited in T. Duchesneau, *Competition in the U.S. Energy Industry* (Cambridge, Mass.: Ballinger, 1975), p. 75.

Table 13   Top 20 Companies' Share of U.S. Coal Production in 1972

RANK	GROUP	TONNAGE (BITUMINOUS AND LIGNITE)	PERCENTAGE OF TOTAL	CUMULATIVE PERCENTAGE
1	Peabody Coal Co.	71,595,310	12.1	12.1
2	Consolidation Coal (O)	64,942,000	11.0	23.1
3	Island Creek Coal (O)	22,605,114	3.8	26.9
4	Pittston Coal	20,639,020	3.5	30.4
5	Amax	16,380,303	2.8	33.2
6	U.S. Steel (S)	16,254,400	2.8	36.0
7	Bethlehem Mines (S)	13,335,245	2.3	38.3
8	Eastern Associated Coal Corp.	12,528,429	2.1	40.4
9	North American Coal Co.	11,991,004	2.0	42.4
10	Old Ben Coal Corp. (O)	11,235,910	1.9	44.3
11	General Dynamics	9,951,263	1.7	46.0
12	Westmoreland Coal Co.	9,063,919	1.5	47.5
13	Pittsburgh & Midway Coal Co. (O)	7,458,791	1.3	48.8
14	Utah International	6,898,262	1.2	50.0
15	American Electric Power	6,329,389	1.1	51.1
16	Western Energy Co.	5,500,700	0.9	52.0
17	Rochester & Pittsburgh	5,137,438	0.9	52.9
18	Valley Camp Coal	4,777,674	0.8	53.7
19	Zeigler Coal Co.	4,201,164	0.7	54.4
20	Midland Coal	3,899,478	0.7	55.1
	Total: Top 20	320,428,813	55.1	
	Total: Others	269,571,187	44.9	
	Total U.S. production	590,000,000		

Note: (O) denotes ownership by an oil company.
       (S) denotes ownership by a steel company.

Source: T. Duchesneau, *Competition in the U.S. Energy Industry* (Cambridge, Mass.: Ballinger, 1975), p. 75.

Kennecott Copper. Steel companies are among the nation's largest coal consumers, and many steel companies are substantial coal producers; U.S. Steel and Bethlehem Steel were the nation's sixth and seventh largest producers in 1972. Some electric utilities (e.g., American Electric Power and Duke Power) produce a significant fraction of their coal needs. And several oil companies also are substantial coal producers.

Apart from this lack of concentration, there are two additional reasons for concluding that coal producers have little or no monopoly power. First, most coal is consumed by electric utilities and steel companies. These companies are large and sophisticated consumers that have the incentive and the means to search for the best buy. Rather than meekly accepting prices quoted by coal companies, they actively solicit competitive bids. Moreover, because many electric utilities and steel companies are themselves substantial coal producers, they would respond to monopoly prices by expanding their own production. Second, the United States has enormous undeveloped but economic coal reserves owned by federal and state governments, several Indian tribes, and the large western land grant railroads. Most of these undeveloped reserves have not been leased, but when they are, many newcomers are likely to enter the coal business.

A firm can enter an industry either by starting its own grass-roots operation or by acquiring an existing firm. Grass roots entry increases the number of firms in the industry and hence, theoretically, heightens competition. Although oil companies have used both methods to enter the coal business, and although no evidence suggests that their presence has reduced competition, those oil companies—Continental, Occidental, SOHIO, and Gulf—that are now the largest coal producers all took the acquisition route.

Because petroleum products can substitute for coal in many uses, oil company coal acquisitions might be opposed on the grounds that they really are horizontal mergers violating Section 7 of the Clayton Act. But if this argument is correct, the crude and refined oil market-share data in Tables 9 and 12 actually overstate the importance of the largest oil companies in the combined coal-oil market; thus, the already low probability that the large oil companies can set monopoly prices is really even lower.

Available evidence on the oil industry's profitability also supports the inference that it is competitive. Between 1963 and 1973, most American oil companies' profits, judged by the most common measure—the after-tax rate of return on equity investments—were below the average for all United States industrial firms.[26] Of course, in 1973–74, oil company profits rose sharply, but even then, they were only slightly higher than the average earned by all United States manufacturing industries; and in the last quarter of 1974, they began falling. Unusually high accounting profits that persist for only a one- or two-year time span, in the midst of unanticipated supply shortages, are not evidence of monopoly.

Professor Edward Mitchell of the University of Michigan recently calculated oil company stockholders' profits over two periods, 1953–74 and 1960–74. He concluded that

> An investment of $1,000 in the American international oil companies, or 14 domestic refiners, or 2 domestic producers whose stock was listed on the major stock exchanges would have left the investor worse off than an investment of $1,000 in the S & P [Standard and Poor] 500 Stock Composite Index. Oil company stockholders have not reaped monopoly profits. Indeed, they have faired somewhat worse than the average owner of common stock.[27]

In a 1973 report, the Federal Trade Commission adopted a line of reasoning that had been favored for a number of years by some oil industry critics—that "the major oil companies in general and the eight largest majors in particular have engaged in conduct . . . squeez[ing] independents at both the refining and marketing levels."[28] The ability to squeeze "has its origins in the structural peculiarities of the petroleum industry" which allow the integrated majors to "limit effectively the supply of crude oil to a point which reduces refinery profits to zero. Clearly such a system creates a hazardous existence for independent refiners who have little or no crude production."[29]

To make the charge of squeezing stick, the FTC needed to show that the integrated majors had some special advantages in the market. It cited two such advantages:

1. The oil import quota clearly contributed to profits earned in producing crude oil by elevating prices, but the quota increased profits to the major in another way. The right to import went only to existing refineries. Thus, the major companies . . . were able to purchase oil at the world price as an input for their refineries which produced final product, at elevated domestic prices.[30]

2. Oil depletion allowances [allowed] . . . a crude oil producing firm . . . to subtract from its gross income before taxes an amount equal to 22 percent of its total revenues from crude production. . . . Under this system the major integrated firms have an incentive to seek high crude prices. The high crude prices are, however, a cost to the major firms' refineries. Thus, an increase in crude prices implies an increase in crude profits but a decrease in refinery profits. The integrated oil companies gain because the depletion allowance reduces the tax on crude profits, while refinery profits are not subject to the same advantageous depletion allowance.[31]

Because both oil-import quotas and the depletion allowance have been abolished, they can no longer be used to support the charge of squeezing. More to the point, even when the quotas and the depletion allowance were in effect, the companies did not engage in squeezing, if only because it was never profitable.

The Mandatory Oil Import Quota Program required that valuable oil-import rights be allocated to domestic refiners as a percentage of their total crude oil inputs. But the allocation formula used a sliding scale that gave small refiners a far larger proportion of imports. Hence, the FTC was wrong in claiming that the allocation of oil-import rights enabled the large, integrated majors to squeeze their smaller, independent competitors.

The oil depletion allowance reduced the effective tax rate

on crude oil profits. The FTC maintained that it gave the large, integrated majors an incentive to raise the price of crude oil and thereby divert taxable profits from refining to crude oil operations.

But the FTC's analysis failed to take proper account of the fact that most of the integrated majors are *not* self-sufficient in crude oil, but must buy additional crude oil from independent producers in order to keep their United States refineries running at capacity levels. In 1973, when the oil depletion allowance was 22 percent, profit shifting could have yielded higher after-tax profits only to those companies that produced at least 93 percent of their crude oil needs.[32] Table 14 reproduces the FTC's estimates of crude oil self-sufficiency for the 17 largest integrated American refiners in 1969. Of these integrated giants, only Getty, the sixteenth largest, produced as much as 93 percent of its total domestic needs. If the 16 majors had shifted profits as the FTC suggested, their marginal after-tax losses would have ranged from a low of 3 cents on each dollar of profits shifted by relatively oil-rich Marathon to a high of 48.3 cents on each dollar of profits shifted by relatively oil-poor Standard Oil of Ohio.[33] Even if the depletion allowance were still allowed, none of these companies could be expected to assume the huge losses involved in profit shifting in order to squeeze independent refiners.

Legislation is currently pending to force the integrated oil companies to divest one or more of their major operations. The proponents of divestiture justify their position by reference to obsolete and mistaken studies such as the FTC's regarding quota and tax advantages and to more recent findings that some oil companies made secret payments here and abroad to win political or economic favors. Those who support the bill argue that breaking up the large oil companies will benefit consumers. But it has been estimated that divestiture is likely to result in even higher fuel prices because the elimination of real integration economies will raise oil companies' costs.[34] Moreover, the mere threat of divestiture (and other punitive legislation) apparently has been discouraging oil companies from making investments of the magnitude necessary to help the United States reduce its oil-import dependence.

Table 14   The FTC's Estimates of the Domestic Self-sufficiency of 17 Leading Refiners in 1969

COMPANY	SELF/SUFFICIENCY (PERCENTAGE OF RUNS TO STILLS)
Standard (New Jersey)	87.4
Standard (Indiana)	50.5[a]
Texaco	81.0[b]
Shell	62.1
Standard (California)	68.8[a]
Mobil	42.2[c]
Gulf	87.6[a,d]
ARCO	64.9
Sun	46.7[e]
Union	64.3[a]
Standard (Ohio)	6.7[a]
Phillips	51.8[a]
Ashland[f]	12.6
Continental	64.0
Cities Service	49.9
Getty[g]	137.2[d]
Marathon	88.1

[a]Other liquids included in crude production.
[b]Estimated.
[c]Other liquids included in refinery runs.
[d]Excludes crude processed for company's account.
[e]Crude production includes Canada.
[f]12 months to September 30, 1969.
[g]Includes subsidiaries.

Source: Federal Trade Commission, *PreliminaryFederal Trade Commission Staff Report on Its Investigation of the Petroleum Industry,* 1973, p. 20.

The United States faces several very real energy policy problems requiring serious and sustained public attention: How can we reduce our still-growing dependence on insecure and expensive oil imports? How can we reduce the environmental and health risks attributable to higher production and consumption of domestic fuels such as coal, oil shale, and nuclear power? And how can the United States guarantee American consumers that they will have access to adequate energy supplies without paying unnecessarily high prices?

Both Congress and the President ought to be examining and, at some point, legislating and adopting policies to deal with these issues. The bitter debate over a domestic oil monopoly that appears not to exist has diverted the attention of policymakers from solving real problems.[35]

OIL-IMPORT POLICIES

Even if the United States could cut its oil imports to zero, its oil-poor allies would still be vulnerable to sudden price increases and/or supply interruptions as long as OPEC retained monopoly control over the international crude oil trade. The two opposing strategies of cooperation or confrontation with the oil exporters have been proposed to counter this threat.

Historically, the United States has advocated increased cooperation as a means of reducing international trade barriers. In theory, reducing trade barriers encourages trade and allows each country to produce more of those goods in which it has a "comparative advantage" (i.e., can produce more efficiently than other countries). Increased trade results in a rise in total world output and, necessarily—since each trading country voluntarily engages in trade—a rise in the real GNP of each country. A further political-strategic purpose of increasing international trade has been to prevent those trading countries whose economies are linked to that of the United States from coming under Soviet hegemony.

The assumption that all trading countries must benefit from the growth of trade is valid only if neither buyer nor seller possesses substantial monopoly power. If one trading partner possesses such power, the other partner is justified in adopting restrictive policies, such as tariffs and quotas, designed to reduce the magnitude of trade with the monopolist and its monopoly power. For many years, the United States has strictly limited trade with Communist-bloc countries, setting a precedent for the use of restrictive trade policies with nations that are thought to engage in hostile economic, military, or political acts.

After the OAPEC embargo, the United States repeatedly tried to negotiate lower prices for oil by advancing the argument that lower and stable oil prices are essential to the continued prosperity of both oil exporters and importers. In 1974, the press reported several instances in which a "senior" State Department official felt he had persuaded key Saudi officials of the efficacy of this argument.[36] Published accounts of the December 1975 ministerial meetings of the 27-nation Conference on International Economic Cooperation indicate that, even at that late date, Secretary of State Kissinger was still advancing the thesis that lower oil prices would benefit all nations.[37] But between January 1974 and early 1976, the cost of Saudi marker crude rose from about $8 per barrel to $11.51 per barrel.

Any sustained interruption in the flow of oil imports would be very costly, and no government wants to adopt policies that might precipitate either further price hikes or another embargo. But several academics have pointed to the ultimate futility of failing to challenge the enormous monopoly power OPEC possesses. A year before the embargo, M. A. Adelman wrote:

> Oil supply is threatened by one and only one danger: a concerted shutdown by the OPEC nations. . . . The cartel is only needed, only exists, to thwart the basic condition of massive potential excess capacity—ability to expand output at costs below prices—and prevent it from becoming actual.
>
> Hence lower prices and secure supply are the two sides of the same coin. . . .
>
> The Monopoly may still have its finest hours before it, and prices should rise well into the decade. . . . The important consuming countries show no sign of understanding their plight . . . A private monopoly which extracted $1.5 billion per year from consumers would be denounced and probably destroyed; were they American, some executives would be in jail. An intergovernmental monopoly ten times as big is viewed as a bit of redress by the Third World.

What happens to oil in the 1970s depends altogether on the consuming countries. If they are as slow to learn as they have been, then the projection of $55 billion annual tribute paid the OPEC nations by 1980 may be surpassed.[38]

OPEC is not a politically vulnerable alliance lacking in long-term market strength. The postembargo oil surpluses are already disappearing. Two-thirds of the non-Communist world's oil supplies come from OPEC nations, and only a few countries are known to have reserves sufficient to support long-term production expansion. The total destruction of the oil cartel is probably an impossible dream. Nevertheless, measures to weaken the cartel do appear feasible.

Two general types of economic countermeasures have been suggested to reduce United States reliance on "insecure" oil imports and weaken OPEC's cohesion. The first is a quota limiting oil imports to an acceptable level: The United States would sell the import rights to oil-exporting nations by sealed, confidential, competitive bids.[39] The three principal benefits claimed for this oil quota are that it would gradually reduce United States dependence on imported oil, eliminate a major source of uncertainty for firms considering whether to invest in developing high-cost domestic energy sources (by eliminating the possibility that lower prices for OPEC oil will make these investments unprofitable), and encourage competition among oil exporters planning to sell in the huge United States market.

The productive capacity of the OPEC countries far exceeds current demands (OPEC's surplus capacity was thought to be more than 10 million barrels per day in early 1976), and most "surplus" oil would cost less than $1 per barrel to produce. Accordingly, most oil-importing countries should be eager to sell more oil at current world prices in the American market. But if the United States adopts an oil-import quota, the amount of oil that any exporter can sell in the lucrative American market would be limited to the number of import rights it had purchases from the United States government at an auction in which both the identity of the bidders and their bids would be secret.

The size of the United States market would offer a strong incentive to each oil-exporting country to cut prices indirectly by raising its bids. Once the price of these rights rises to about 10 cents per barrel, this policy should really begin to bite. Over time, low bidders would find their sales in the United States market plummeting. Disgruntled bidders who bid too low at earlier sales would bid higher at subsequent import rights sales. At this point, the exporters of the 6 million to 10 million barrels of oil that the United States imports daily would be forced back into a semicompetitive situation.

The OPEC countries can always emasculate the quota-auction scheme be refraining from bidding for United States oil-imports rights. But those OPEC members—especially Venezuela—that now sell most of their oil in the American market would find such self-denial difficult. Unless OPEC pays compensation to members who suffer a sharp fall in sales, the economic incentive to participate in the quota auction would seem nearly irresistible.

The other type of anti-OPEC economic strategy calls for placing a high tariff on oil imports. An oil tariff would raise domestic fuel prices, thereby reducing energy demand and promoting increased energy production from those domestic sources whose prices were allowed to rise.

One promising variant of the oil tariff involves placing a high tariff on all imports but granting partial or total exemptions for imports from countries that satisfy specific security criteria.[40] The "differential" tariff might work, for example, by dividing the oil-exporting countries into three classes. Secure countries would include Canada and Mexico, countries that share borders with the United States and have never been OPEC members; crude oil imports from these countries would be charged no tariff. Insecure countries might include those that joined in the OAPEC embargo; oil imports from these countries could be charged a high (perhaps $10 per barrel) tariff. Oil imports from all other countries could be charged a lower (perhaps $2 per barrel) tariff. A country could change its tariff classification by offering price or quantity guarantees.

A differential tariff on oil imports would encourage some reduction in United States consumption of oil imports; more important, foment jealousy among those OPEC members who receive different tariff classifications; and offer strong financial inducements for suppliers of secure oil to expand current output and for other suppliers to furnish guarantees to the United States that they are worthy of reclassification into a more favorable tariff category. Those nations that chose to threaten United States oil security would do so knowing that they might be reclassified into a higher tariff category.

The choice facing policymakers is a difficult one. Economic policies such as the quota auction and the differential tariff are essentially forms of economic warfare—steps that are not to be taken lightly. Moreover, many policymakers regard all anti-OPEC economic measures as counterproductive. They argue that substantial reliance on OPEC oil is inevitable for several more years and that the United States should not now adopt a strategy that provokes conflict; instead, it should pursue new modes of linking national economies by fostering international cooperation. Those who advocate anti-OPEC policies rebut this argument by noting that OPEC members have repeatedly raised prices and unilaterally terminated agreements since 1970, and that there is no real basis for international cooperation as long as the exercise of monopoly power is unchecked.

4

The Process of Energy Policymaking

Virtually all assessments of United States energy policy criticize its shortcoming and inadequacies and ascribe them to (1) the inherent complexity of energy problems, which makes the formulation and implementation of an effective, coordinated set of remedial policies impossible; (2) bad or weak leadership—either incompetent or vulnerable to pressures from special interests; or (3) defects in the policymaking process.

If energy problems are too complicated, the United States is simply wasting resources by attempting to develop an effective energy policy. Admittedly, no group of top policymakers can hope to comprehend fully the detailed technical and business issues that those involved in the various phases of the energy industry must address daily. Energy resembles many other policy issues in this respect. Policymakers may reasonably be expected to possess a general comprehension of the United States' present energy problems and of the virtues and defects of the major energy policy tools.

If bad leadership or irresponsibility lies at the root of most energy policy failures, then the obvious remedy is to change the leadership. But criticism of United States energy policy has been widespread and vigorous for the past 50 years, during which top-level leadership has changed several times. No doubt, some energy policymakers have been incompetent and others have acquiesced too readily to the selfish demands of special interest groups. Partisan politics and rivalries between the executive and legislative branches also have undoubtedly distorted policy formulation. But changing leadership cannot eliminate these distortions; they are symptoms of weakness in the policymaking process itself. The energy policymaking process suffers from four serious, interrelated, but remediable defects:

1. The failure of policymakers to articulate the principal goals of energy policy and to establish priorities for achieving them; the result is a wasteful misallocation of resources.
2. The fragmentation of energy policy decision making. No single decision-making unit has ultimate responsibility for energy policy. Various agencies work without coordination and frequently at cross-purposes.
3. The ambiguity of the basic economic, environmental, political, and technological constraints on policy and the tendency of these constraints to change without warning.
4. The politicization of debate over energy policy and the tendency to dwell on false or emotionally charged issues.

THE ENERGY POLICYMAKING APPARATUS

Businesses typically attempt to coordinate multifaceted operations by setting up an administrative structure in which line departments, charged with devising and implementing solutions to specific problems, report to a staff that has ultimate responsibility for overall policy coordination and supervision. The federal government contains literally hundreds of departments, agencies, bureaus, commissions, and offices that have line responsibility for drafting, implementing, and enforcing laws and regulations covering specific energy areas. But no agency of government performs the staff function effectively.

Congress and the President share ultimate responsibility for determining both the scope of United States energy policy and the general design of specific policy measures. Formally,

Congress delegates this responsibility to upwards of 50 committees and subcommittees. No congressional body coordinates the efforts of these groups.

In the executive branch, the Energy Resources Council (ERC) has formal responsibility for overall design and supervision of United States energy policy. In addition to several key presidential aides, the ERC's membership includes the heads of the major executive departments and agencies most involved in the administration of day-to-day energy policy—some 23 prestigious individuals. But the ERC has neither sufficient permanent manpower nor sufficient day-to-day input from its members to coordinate policymaking effectively.[1] Many of the more important agencies involved in making energy policy have therefore pursued goals that conformed to their own assessment of United States energy priorities and concerns.

Interior Department   Before the late 1960s, the Interior Department was the most important source of United States energy policy. Its line divisions, such as the Bureau of Mines, the U.S. Geological Survey, the Bureau of Land Management, and the (now defunct) Office of Oil and Gas, were responsible for implementing and monitoring federal policies regarding fossil fuel energy research, leasing of federal lands for energy production and transmission, and regulation of oil imports.

Critics have often complained that the Interior Department is tied too closely to the domestic fossil fuel interests. One tie has come under especially severe attack: Through membership in the quasi-official National Petroleum Council, top oil industry executives have the unique privilege of being able to advise, inform, and make recommendations to the Secretary of the Interior on any matter relating to petroleum or the petroleum industry. To prevent the interests of the industry from coming to represent the national interest, some observers have advocated abolishing the National Petroleum Council and placing severe strictures on the government's hiring of former oil company employees. But such reforms may be too harsh. First, as long as the public is aware of the special role played by the National Petroleum Council, official advice from that source is unlikely to be accorded undue weight. Moreover, it may be preferable to have the oil industry's policy input take place through official rather than unofficial channels. Second, experienced employees well versed in the different phases of the oil business are absolutely essential if the United States is to have a well-designed energy policy. Therefore, rather than adopting policies that make it nearly impossible to recruit such employees, it would seem preferable to design rules of ethics that prevent abuses. If such rules cannot be designed, and if the government is unable to train its own experts, it is unlikely that the nation's energy policies can be both highly detailed and efficient.

Because of its long-standing involvement in energy matters, the Interior Department should logically have played a leading role in formulating and implementing policies to solve our post-1969 energy problems. But making major changes in existing energy policies clearly required reasonably broad-based public support. Interior was too closely identified with domestic energy interests to assume this politically sensitive task. Today, most important energy policy decisions are made elsewhere. However, because of its expertise and experience—especially in assessing the United States' energy resources and in managing the public lands—the Interior Department continues to play a key role in implementing those policies that are adopted.

Treasury Department Historically, the Treasury Department has been concerned with three energy policy issues: the balance-of-payments implications of the United States' rising oil imports, the efficiency and equity effects of the tax benefits granted to domestic energy companies, and the implications for federal revenues of additional sales of federal mineral land leases. But under the leadership of George Shultz, Treasury extended its authority. In 1973, the Treasury Department took the lead in molding the Nixon administration's position on such key issues as oil-import policy, proposals for rationing of oil supplies that were scarce because of the OAPEC embargo, and charges that the nation's oil problems were the result of a conspiracy among oil companies. In his role as presidential counselor, Shultz also had considerable influence over the policy decisions of Interior, Commerce, and what was to become the Federal Energy Administration. With his departure, Treasury lost some of its dominance over United States energy policymaking, although its responsibilities remain greater than they were before his appointment.

State Department   The economic, military, and political issues posed by both the increasing dependence of the United States and its allies on oil imported from the OPEC countries and the growing concern over the dangers stemming from the worldwide proliferation of radioactive materials have guaranteed the State Department a growing role in the formulation of United States energy policy. The success of American efforts to maintain peace in the Middle East will influence the course of United States energy policy for many years to come. Unfortunately, the State Department under Henry Kissinger was a highly individualized operation that lacked experienced senior staff capable of analyzing the economic consequences of future energy policies.

Defense Department   The goal of reducing threats to the security of the United States has provided the principal justification for many of the United States' energy policies. It might also have justified giving the Defense Department a key role in setting United States energy policy, but in fact, the Defense Department has not participated in making such important energy policy decisions as the determination of an acceptable level for United States oil imports and the decision to press construction of the trans-Alaskan pipeline. Others made these decisions and merely asked Defense to add its prestigious endorsement. The Defense Department seems not to have either the inclination or the expertise to alter this state of affairs in the foreseeable future.

Commerce Department   The Commerce Department views its mission as promoting improved efficiency for all American commerce and industry. In general, American business has been able to rely on Commerce to press its interests within the executive branch. In energy policy matters, Commerce has been most closely identified with two positions. First, since the Interior Department represents the interests of energy producers and landowners, Commerce seeks to represent the interests of industrial energy consumers and has been an especially strong supporter of all efforts by petrochemical companies to get cheaper petroleum as a raw material for their manufacturing. Second, Commerce has long been an active proponent of increased trade with the Soviet Union, viewing crude oil and liquefied natural gas as two of the Soviet Union's potentially most valuable exports. Since the OAPEC embargo, Commerce has tried to take the lead in promoting greater energy conservation by business. (In practice, it has had to share this mission with the Federal Energy Administration and the Energy Research and Development Administration.) But despite these efforts, Commerce plays a subsidiary role in shaping United States energy policy, a role that seems appropriate given the narrowness of the department's political base in the area.

Federal Power Commission   The Federal Power Commission's principal assignment is to regulate interstate shipments and sales of natural gas and electricity in order to mitigate present and anticipated shortages of natural gas and, if possible, to forestall future shortages of electricity. But Congress has mandated that the FPC set below-market-clearing price ceilings on natural gas. In recent years, a majority of the Commissioners have sought to offset these controls by endorsing policies aimed at reducing the supply-and-demand distortions they cause. Because most electricity sales are not subject to FPC regulation, the agency has been unable to have much effect in this area. Like several other agencies and departments, the FPC seeks to expand its energy duties by becoming a promoter of energy conservation and research and development.

Environmental Protection Agency   The Environmental Protection Agency, established in 1970 to consolidate federal environmental activities, drafts and enforces a great variety of standards designed to reduce environmental damage. Some of these standards (e.g., emission standards for motor vehicles and stationary power plants) have resulted in higher energy consumption; others have made it difficult to use certain abundant domestic fuel supplies (notably, high-sulphur coal). In addition, the EPA sponsors an extensive energy-related research and development program, which it describes as being designed to develop

> a sound technical and scientific basis for ensuring (1) adequate protection of human health, welfare, ecosystem, and social goals; (2) environmental protection necessary to facilitate the use of energy supplies, with particular emphasis on domestic fuels; (3) implementation of energy system initiatives without delays caused by inadequate and insufficient environmental impact data; (4) development of appropriate cost-effective control technologies for emerging energy systems; and (5) assessment of the environmental implications of energy conservation measures in order to maximize the energy savings and minimize the associated adverse impacts.[2]

Although the EPA has important responsibilities and the ability to impede the development of large new domestic energy supplies, nevertheless it is a peripheral source of present United States energy policy. Other federal agencies seldom consult the EPA on energy matters, and the public's fears of worsening energy shortages may ultimately curtail the EPA's power to combat energy-related polluting activities.

Nuclear Regulatory Commission   The Nuclear Regulatory Commission was established in January 1975 to take over the Atomic Energy Commission's responsibility for licensing nuclear facilities and conducting reactor-safety research. In addition, the NRC was to conduct research on the protection of nuclear materials and the feasibility of an agency to monitor nuclear security and to initiate an energy site survey. The NRC also has the critical and thankless task of devising an acceptable, economical trade-off between increased reliance on nuclear power and public health and safety.

Energy Research and Development Administration The Energy Research and Development Administration provides a channel for the government's efforts to encourage technical development and, ultimately, commercial production of promising future fuels. Like NRC, ERDA is an offshoot of the Atomic Energy Commission (AEC). It operates huge national laboratories, such as Oak Ridge and Argonne, and produces all of the nation's enriched uranium. The largest portion of ERDA's research and development budget is devoted to programs formerly conducted by the AEC, including demonstrations of the feasibility of breeder reactors and high-temperature gas-cooled reactors and sponsorship of research on fusion. In addition, ERDA is also preparing to begin extensive research and development on solar and geothermal power and to develop advanced power systems such as magnetohydrodynamics and fuel cells. It also is sponsoring research to demonstrate the commercial feasibility of coal synthetics and programs designed to improve the recovery of crude oil and natural gas from known high-cost sources. The agency also has made a commitment to conduct research on new methods of conserving energy by promoting more efficient methods of consumption. The principal question facing ERDA is whether it will succeed in broadening its horizon beyond its historical role of expanding the use of nuclear power.

Federal Energy Administration The Federal Energy Administration was established in 1974 as the successor of a long line of agencies, departments, offices, committees, and individuals charged with channeling the executive branch's efforts to deal with the energy problem. Initially, many observers hoped the FEA would provide oversight and coordination for United States energy policy. But the FEA has confined itself largely to performing three specific tasks: (1) administering the horrendously complicated regulations fixing prices of crude oil and most refined petroleum products, (2) administering the old-oil entitlements program, and (3) developing and analyzing data that will help the United States to develop comprehensive, long-range energy policies.

Maintaining that it is the only governmental body concentrating exclusively on remedying United States energy problems, the FEA has tried, with mixed success, to expand its purview to other areas. Its publicity department, which employs 112 of the agency's 3,700 employees, issues hundreds of releases about the gravity of the energy problem, the desirability of expanding United States energy production, and the virtues of frugality in energy use.[3] Assistant administrators for International Energy Affairs, Conservation and the Environment, Energy Resource Development, and Regulatory Programs run offices whose functions largely duplicate those already performed by other government departments or agencies. New offices have recently been established to explain the natural gas shortage to Americans and to advocate expanded use of nuclear power. The Topsy-like growth of the FEA has been attacked from all sides. Such diverse citizens as Ralph Nader, Charles DiBona (vice-president of the American Petroleum Institute and formerly President Nixon's chief energy adviser), and Treasury Secretary William Simon (director of FEA's immediate predecessor, the Federal Energy Office) have been quoted as stating that the FEA should be abolished.[4]

THE SCOPE OF ENERGY POLICYMAKING

Relatively little is known about the economic, environmental, political, and technical conditions that will affect the implementation of all important energy policies. It is poor strategy to adopt highly detailed, inflexible policies whose success depends on the occurrence of a specific and perhaps unlikely chain of events.

The prospective development of many important sources of energy will require massive investments and take a long time. Thus, investment decisions made this year will affect both the volume and the cost of the United States' post-1985 domestic energy supplies. Future energy supplies are more likely to be inadequate or unnecessarily costly if public officials who are ignorant of the relevant economic and technical constraints or must downplay their importance in order to accommodate political pressures attempt to engage in detailed energy planning.

Too much indecision or ambiguity by policymakers can also create costly uncertainty for energy consumers and producers. A glaring example of the costs of indecision is the long delay in bringing oil from Alaska's giant Prudhoe Bay field into commercial production. And frequent changes in established energy policies can lead to obsolescence of some large capital investments. For example, in 1975, the Federal Energy Administration adopted regulations forcing the owners of 32 oil-fueled electricity plants to spend an estimated $260 million to convert to burning coal. Many of these plants had earlier spent millions switching from coal to oil in order to satisfy federal clean air standards.

Objective policy studies can make an important contribution to improving the quality of the energy policy debate by providing estimates of the net costs and benefits of different policy initiatives and by identifying issues that are extraneous. The fact that nearly all extant scholarly studies on United States energy policymaking have been highly critical suggests that relatively simple and flexible policies that rely heavily on economic and technical signals as expressed in the marketplace may serve the public more effectively and equitably than complex policies requiring intricately detailed planning, implementation, and enforcement.

CONGRESS AND THE PRESIDENT

Congress and the President must somehow perform successfully four tasks if the United States is to have a well-designed, effective energy policy:

1. They must determine the appropriate goals for national energy policy and assign priorities to them. This assignment cannot be delegated to "experts." The American public is sharply divided over energy policy issues. Producers and citizens from the major energy-producing states tend to favor policies that encourage

greater energy output by allowing higher energy prices; consumers and citizens from energy-consuming states, especially energy-short New England, vociferously oppose such policies. The public utterances of the different interest groups do reflect significant value differences regarding the allocation of costs and benefits stemming from our energy policies. Policymakers have the responsibility of listening to and somehow synthesizing the views of the public. Being somewhat more accessible to the people than is the executive branch, Congress may be more adept than the President at performing this vital task.

2. They must design a program to achieve these policy goals. Congress' lack of specific expertise in energy matters explains why it cannot design a coherent set of detailed energy policies. Therefore, the chief congressional duty ought to be to pass legislation that either mandates in a very general way what types of energy policies the executive branch should initiate or abolishes present policies that Congress judges to have failed. In practice, Congress has not been content with playing this rather limited, statesmanlike role. Instead, it has legislated or is contemplating legislating quite detailed laws in a variety of areas ranging from strip-mining of coal, to mandatory standards for automobile emissions and mileage, to crude oil price controls, to restructuring the method of leasing Outer Continental Shelf oil lands, to establishing a federal oil and gas company to forcing the large, integrated oil companies to divest some of their operations. Regardless of one's assessment of the merits of the goals of these different pieces of legislation, it is difficult to imagine that Congress can design policies to achieve them in a relatively efficient fashion. This task is better left to the executive branch.

3. They must implement and enforce specific energy policies. Because Congress has no line divisions, the President must assume this responsibility.

4. They must audit the policies they have adopted and evaluate their effectiveness in terms of their stated goals. Congress can make a substantial contribution to

improving United States energy policy by holding oversight hearings at which the key executive agencies must justify their actual performance. Such hearings would offer interested parties and independent (i.e., nongovernment and nonindustry) experts the most visible public forum for expressing their views. Given the adversary relationship that always exists to some degree between the executive and legislative branches, it is unlikely that bad or ineffective federal policies will escape unscathed from congressional review.

CENTRALIZATION OF ENERGY POLICYMAKING

Proposals to assign sole responsibility for the design and implementation of the executive branch's policy responsibilities to one cabinet-level agency have the charm of simplicity and have been endorsed repeatedly by top government officials.[5] But the multifaceted nature of present energy problems argues against such extensive streamlining. For example, the United States would be unable to carry out a coherent foreign policy if the State Department were not allowed to consider the international ramifications of a variety of domestic and international energy policies, and the Treasury Department must have broad authority to consider energy when drafting tax legislation. The history of the Federal Energy Administration, which established offices of international energy affairs, regulatory programs, and others, suggests that a new energy department may find it necessary to develop expertise similar to that already found in other departments and increase rather than decrease duplication.

Moreover, the desirability of many energy policies is legitimately debatable. The United States' unsatisfactory experience with the Atomic Energy Commission—responsible both for promoting the commercial development of nuclear power and for making sure this development was safe—suggests that a single agency may not be able to take account of conflicting viewpoints and that an agency charged with assuring the development of adequate domestic energy supplies may give short shrift to the interests of environmentalists and, perhaps, consumer groups.

In any case, enabling one agency to perform the array of energy-related administrative chores presently supervised by the 23 high-level officials who are members of the ERC would take several years, during which time indecision would reign until the affected bureaucrats learned their roles in the new organization.

The delegation of the President's executive authority to a "National Energy Administrator" represents a more modest alternative to consolidating all (or most) energy policy responsibilities within one department. This approach would keep the present division of the executive branch's energy policy line responsibilities essentially unchanged but fix with the Administrator ultimate responsibility for determining policy priorities and requiring interdepartmental coordination. But the National Energy Administrator would almost certainly be ineffective unless given the strongest possible presidential support—hence, he should work out of the White House and report directly to the President. Speedy decision making would be possible only if the Administrator had unquestioned authority to speak for the President on all energy issues, but he would also be required to consult regularly with an informed, broadly representative, and prestigious advisory group. Finally, every effort would be made to keep the Administrator from getting bogged down in the detailed day-to-day administrative problems that should be the responsibility of the line departments.

Congress and the President share responsibility for the design of United States energy policy. Energy policy formulation is subject to long delays, contradictions, and duplication at least in part because congressional responsibility in this area is divided among scores of different committees. Some reduction in the number of committees is almost certainly desirable. But reducing the number of congressional committees with energy responsibilities carries some risks. First, it might narrow the forums available for debate. Second, it might not alter Congress' tendency to pass highly detailed laws (which have allowed little executive discretion) without adequate consideration of the cost-effectiveness of specific provisions. Indeed, the stronger committees that survive such a reorganization would be likely to write even more detailed legislation. Third, there are limits as to how much consolidation is feasible. Energy issues impinge on several other areas. For example, an energy committee is probably not the ideal place to consider such issues as the foreign policy implications of United States international energy policies or the appropriate taxes for oil companies. Consolidation of committees would not eliminate conflicts of this sort.

Many energy policy problems arise because of a lack of communication and coordination between the executive and legislative branches. A joint congressional/presidential committee might discuss the nature and relative importance of present United States energy problems and the efficacy of different policy tools. Such a committee has no modern analogue. Of course, to be effective, it would require a real commitment on the part of both the President and the congressional leadership. Nevertheless, any proposal for alleviating some of the rancor between the two branches of government deserves serious consideration.

Notes

The author was assisted in his research by Barbara Hobbie.

Chapter 1

[1] OAPEC is composed of the Arab members of the Organization of Petroleum Exporting Countries (OPEC). All major oil-exporting countries except Canada are OPEC members. Members of the OAPEC subgroup accounted for roughly 60 percent of OPEC's sales just prior to the start of the 1973–74 OAPEC oil embargo.

[2] "Aramco Sees Rapid Restoration of Crude," *Oil and Gas Journal*, January 28, 1974, p. 94.

[3] Total United States energy expenditures are inferred from statistics presented in the *Survey of Current Business*, January 1976. The estimate of total United States energy consumption in 1976 is from "Pirnic Sees Rising Energy, Oil Demand," *Oil and Gas Journal*, November 24, 1975, p. 30.

[4] Primary energy is frequently converted into more useful forms. For example, oil refiners convert crude oil into refined oil products such as heating oils and gasoline; and electric utilities convert residual fuel oil, coal, natural gas, and enriched uranium into electricity.

[5] A report published in May 1975 by an MIT study group concludes:

> The U.S. economy entered a deep recession after the embargo and price increase of 1973–74. Though energy problems are given a large role in popular accounts of the recession, experts in macroeconomics generally find that they are of minor importance. The prevailing expert view is that the current recession is basically similar to earlier recessions in resulting from a reduction in aggregate *demand*. Contractionary monetary and fiscal policies are the fundamental cause of the current recession, in this view. The embargo and price increase brought about an unusually difficult choice for policy-makers between high levels of inflation and high rates of unemployment, but they could have chosen a more expansionary policy and thereby prevented the recession. The recession should be viewed as the method chosen by policymakers to deal with inflation (only part of which is attributable to the oil price increase), not an inevitable result of the embargo.

The MIT study report also states that available macroeconomic models are too highly aggregated to permit analysis of the impact of energy problems on the general economy. MIT Energy Laboratory Policy Study Group, *The FEA Project Independence Report: An Analytical Review and Evaluation* (Cambridge, Mass.: MIT, 1975), pp. 5-3 and 5-5. Also see Arthur Okun, "Unemployment and Output in 1974," *Brookings Papers on Economic Activity*, vol. 2, 1974.

Chapter 2

This chapter follows closely the presentation in Chapters 3 and 4 of Richard B. Mancke, *Squeaking By: U.S. Energy Policy since the Embargo* (New York: Columbia University Press, 1976).

[1]*Paying for Energy: Report of the Twentieth Century Fund Task Force on the International Oil Crisis* (New York: McGraw-Hill, 1975), pp. 48–50.

[2]Meadows, Donella et al., *The Limits to Growth* (New York: New American Library, 1972).

[3]*New York Times*, November 8, 1973, p. 1.

[4]Federal Energy Administration, *Project Independence Report* (Washington, D.C.: U.S. Government Printing Office, 1974).

[5]For example, see (a) MIT Energy Laboratory Policy Study Group, op. cit.; (b) Mancke, *Squeaking By*, chap. 3; (c) Statement of C. C. Garvin, Chairman of Exxon, to the Texas Mid-Continent Oil and Gas Association; reported in "U.S. Self-Sufficiency by 1985 Doubted," *Oil and Gas Journal*, October 27, 1975, p. 43.

[6]Federal Energy Administration, *National Energy Outlook, 1976* (Washington, D.C.: U.S. Government Printing Office, 1976).

[7]Inferred from M.A. Adelman, *The World Petroleum Market* (Baltimore: The Johns Hopkins University Press, 1972), p. 77 and adjusted to take account of inflation after discussion with a senior official of a major international oil company.

[8]J. W. Devanney, R. J. Stewart, and R. Ciliano, *A Preliminary Estimate of the Domestic Supply Curve of Oil from Conventional Sources*, Martingdale Report to Mathematica for the Environmental Protection Agency, February 20, 1975, pp. 6–7.

[9]Total wells drilled in the United States were 26,703 in 1970; 27,602 in 1973; and 38,904 in 1975. The acceleration of exploration and development appears to be due to the sharp rise in prices of the roughly 40 percent of all domestic crude oil classified as new, released, or stripper and not subject to price controls until early 1976. Prices of this oil rose from about $6 on the embargo's eve to about $14 by year-end 1975. The Energy Policy and Conservation Act of 1975 requires a partial rollback of these exempt crude oil prices (initially to about $11.28 per barrel) and mandates that all crude oil price controls are to be phased out over a 40-month period. However, in light of the current anti-oil-industry political environment, many oil company executives privately express skepticism that this provision of the act will be carried out.

[10]Some idea of the relatively high productivity of the United States' OCS lands may be inferred from the following data. In 1969, total crude oil production from leased federal OCS lands averaged nearly 61 barrels per acre. In

contrast, total crude oil production from leased federal onshore lands averaged only 3 barrels per acre.

[11]Deduced from calculations presented in Richard B. Mancke, *A Method for Estimating Future Crude Oil Production from the United States' Outer Continental Shelf* (Medford, Mass.: Fletcher School of Law and Diplomacy, Tufts University, 1975).

[12]Geologist M. King Hubbert has been the most persuasive proponent of this thesis. See M. King Hubbert, *U.S. Energy Resources, A Review of 1972*, in U.S. Senate Committee on Interior and Insular Affairs, *U.S. Energy Resources: A Review of 1972* (Washington, D.C.: U.S. Government Printing Office, 1974), pp. 1–201.

[13]J. W. Devanney, *The OCS Petroleum Pie* (Cambridge, Mass.: MIT Department of Ocean Engineering, 1974).

[14]Don E. Kash et al., *Energy under the Oceans: A Technology Assessment of Outer Continental Shelf Oil and Gas Operations* (Norman, Okla.: University of Oklahoma Press, 1973).

[15]Ibid., p. 117.

[16]Max Blumer et al., "A Small Oil Spill," *Environment*, March 1971, p. 7.

[17]For elaboration, see Mancke, *Squeaking By*, chap. 4.

[18]J. W. Devanney and R. J. Stewart, *Analysis of Oil Spill Statistics*, Report to the Council of Environmental Quality, MIT Sea Grant Report No. 74-20, pp. 118–119 and 124; Kash et al., op. cit., pp. 241–243.

[19]Kenneth O. Emery, "Offshore Oil: Technology ... and Emotion," *Technology Review*, February 1976, p. 35.

[20]OCS production in the Gulf of Alaska raises two special environmental concerns. First, because low temperatures cause slower evaporation and, in winter, lack of sunshine retards photochemical oxidation, spills in Alaskan waters are likely to retain their toxicity for longer periods than spills in other OCS waters. Second, the Gulf of Alaska is a region with extremely adverse physical conditions: earthquakes, undersea landslides, tidal waves, and extraordinarily high winds and seas.

[21]It should be pointed out that if no oil discoveries were made between now and 1985, total United States production of crude oil and natural gas liquids (including that from Prudhoe Bay) would total only about 7.5 million barrels per day, or about three-quarters what it is today.

[22]Federal Energy Administration, *National Energy Outlook, 1976*, pp. xxx and 131.

[23]The United States' mineable coal reserves are sufficient to last more than 800 years at current production rates. Also, coal's share of the total United States energy market has fallen from more than 90 percent in 1900 to only 17 percent in 1974.

[24]Edwin McDowell, "The Big Battle over Scrubbers," *Wall Street Journal*, February 7, 1975, p. 6.

[25]Les Gapay, "Nuclear Energy Centers Feasible and Practical," *Wall Street Journal*, December 26, 1975, p. 10.

[26]But an explosion due to a power surge resulting from a mishandling of a control rod killed three workers at the SL-1 experimental reactor near Idaho Falls, Idaho, in 1961. See Ralph Lapp, *A Citizen's Guide to Nuclear Power*, (Washington, D.C.: New Republic Inc., 1974), p. 18.

[27]David Burnham, "AEC Files Show Efforts to Conceal Safety Perils," *New York Times*, November 10, 1974, p. 1.

[28]U.S. Nuclear Regulatory Commission, *Reactor Safety Study: An Assessment of the Accident Risks in U.S. Commercial Nuclear Power Plants*, WASH-1400 (Washington, D.C.: U.S. Nuclear Regulatory Commission, 1975), p. 8 of Executive Summary.

[29]Ibid., pp. 9–10.

[30]David Brand, "Nuclear Safety Debate Rages over Reliability of Emergency Systems," *Wall Street Journal*, July 9, 1975, p. 1.

[31]American Physical Society Study Group on Reactor Safety, in *Review of Modern Physics*, vol. 47, suppl. 1, Summer 1975, p. 85.

[32]Ibid., pp. S49–S51. The final WASH-1400 report raised some of its fatality estimates as a result of the American Physical Society study.

[33]Based on discussions with Professor Ernest Klema.

[34]David F. Salisbury, "Quarantining Plutonium," *Technology Review*, January 1976, pp. 4–5.

[35]Robert Gillette, "The Age of Nuclear Energy: A Prolonged Adolescence," *New York Times*, February 15, 1976, section 4, p. 1.

[36]Federal Energy Administration, *Project Independence Report*, p. 127.

[37]Federal Energy Administration, *National Energy Outlook, 1976*, Table V-2, p. 243.

[38]Federal Energy Administration, *National Energy Outlook, 1976*, p. 232.

[39]The FEA projects that electric power generation, which provided 28 percent of the nation's energy in 1974, will provide 37 percent in 1990. "FEA: Prices Hold Key to Energy Future," *Oil and Gas Journal*, March 15, 1976, p. 60.

[40]Inferred from *Project Independence Report*, Table AII-I, appendix AII, p. 60.

[41]These illustrations are based on the discussion in Richard B. Mancke, *The Failure of U.S. Energy Policy* (New York: Columbia University Press, 1974), pp. 4–5.

Chapter 3

[1]Milton Friedman and Robert Roosa, *The Balance of Payments: Free versus Fixed Exchange Rates* (Washington, D.C.: American Enterprise Institute, 1967), p. 1.

[2]15 U.S. Code, 717 Note 3, 1964.

[3]Ibid.

[4]But the natural gas industry has thousands of firms; the largest of these firms accounts for less than 10 percent of total industry sales, and entry by new firms is easy. Most academic economists therefore believe that the monopoly power argument was and is fallacious. For a recent summary of academic economists' views about natural gas wellhead price regulation, see Patricia E. Starratt, *The Natural Gas Shortage and the Congress* (Washington, D.C.: American Enterprise Institute, 1975).

[5]But most comprehensive studies fail to support the premise that natural gas supplies are not price-responsive. Using 1950s and early 1960s data, these studies conclude (too optimistically, it now appears) that United States natural gas supplies were roughly unit-elastic in the long run. See E. Erickson and R. Spann, "Supply Response in a Regulated Industry: The Case of Natural Gas," *Bell Journal of Economics and Management Science*,

Spring 1971, pp. 94–121 and J. D. Khazzoom, "The FPC Staff's Econometric Model of Natural Gas Supply in the United States," *Bell Journal of Economics and Management Science*, Spring 1971.

[6]A more recent and comprehensive study also concludes that natural gas supplies have considerable price responsiveness. See Paul MacAvoy and Robert Pyndyck, *The Economics of the Natural Gas Shortage* (Washington, D.C.: American Enterprise Institute, 1975).

[7]For a full text of the bill, see Bureau of National Affairs, *Energy Users Report*, Special Supplement, Conference Report on S. 622, December 11, 1975.

[8]For a description of the FEA's proposals, see "FEA Spells Out New Tier Price Regs," *Oil and Gas Journal*, January 12, 1976, pp. 43–45. The FEA also asked for comments on several proposals designed either to improve the equity of the new regulations or to make them more efficient. These proposals have been revised subsequently.

[9]If the FEA abolished the present two-tier system of crude oil prices and instead enforced a $7.66 per barrel average price for all oil, an entitlements program would not be necessary.

[10]Federal Energy Administration, *National Energy Outlook, 1976*, p. xxvii.

[11]Companies frequently pay lease bonuses, royalties, and severance taxes to either the landowner or the state before they can produce and sell oil from any given field. Although these payments are obviously real costs to the oil producer, the economist terms them "rents." Unlike, for example, retail store overhead costs, which are included in the retail selling price of a given item, rents are themselves determined by the spread between production cost and selling price.

[12]MIT Energy Laboratory Policy Study Group, op. cit., p. 5-1.

[13]S. 622, Title III.

[14]Energy Policy Project of the Ford Foundation, op. cit. The report of Ford's EPP has been harshly criticized by many economists on the grounds that it downplays economic factors. (See especially Institute for Contemporary Studies, *No Time to Confuse* [San Francisco, 1975]). Thus Ford's recognition of the primacy of higher prices as a method of promoting conservation is especially significant.

[15]*White House Fact Sheet on the Energy Independence Authority*, October 10, 1975.

[16]Ibid., p. 4.

[17]Ibid.

[18]MIT Energy Laboratory Policy Study Group, op. cit., p. 8-1.

[19]This section relies heavily on material that appears in Richard B. Mancke, *Squeaking By,* chap. 7 and Richard B. Mancke, "Competition in the Oil Industry," in Edward J. Mitchell (ed.), *Vertical Integration in the Oil Industry* (Washington, D.C.: American Enterprise Institute, 1976).

[20]James McKie, "Market Structure and Uncertainty in Oil and Gas Exploration," *Quarterly Journal of Economics*, LXXXIV, 1960, p. 569.

[21]M. A. Adelman, *The World Petroleum Market* (Baltimore: The Johns Hopkins University Press, 1972), pp. 105–106.

[22]Leonard Weiss, *Deposition for* U.S. v. I.B.M., U.S. District Court, Southern District of New York, June 11, 1974, pp. 354–355.

[23]Edward Erickson and Robert Spann, *Entry, Risk Sharing and Competition in Joint Ventures for Offshore Petroleum Exploration*, unpublished, December 1975, pp. 33–34.

[24] Paul MacAvoy and Robert Pyndyck, *Price Controls and the Natural Gas Shortage* (Washington, D.C.: American Enterprise Institute, 1975) and Stephen Breyer and Paul MacAvoy, *Energy Regulation by the Federal Power Commission* (Washington, D.C.: Brookings, 1974).

[25] Paul MacAvoy, *Price Formation in Natural Gas Fields* (New Haven, Conn.: Yale University Press, 1962), pp. 252–253.

[26] See *Oil and Gas Journal*, February 19, 1974, p. 38. For more elaboration see Edward Erickson and Robert Spann, "The U.S. Petroleum Industry," in Edward Erickson and Leonard Waverman, *The Energy Question*, vol. 2 (Toronto, Canada: University of Toronto Press, 1974), pp. 6–12.

[27] See statement of Edward Mitchell, *Hearings before the Subcommittee on Antitrust and Monopoly, U.S. Senate Committee on the Judiciary*, January 22, 1976, p. 60 of xeroxed submission.

[28] Federal Trade Commission, "Preliminary Federal Trade Commission Staff Report on Its Investigation of the Petroleum Industry," in U.S. Senate Permanent Subcommittee on Investigation of the Committee on Government Operations, *Investigation of the Petroleum Industry* (Washington, D.C.: U.S. Government Printing Office, 1973), p. 43.

[29] Ibid., pp. 17 and 43.

[30] Ibid., p. 15.

[31] Ibid., p. 17.

[32] Proof.

Let

t = the fraction of gross profits retained by a large integrated major after paying all federal profit taxes

R = the integrated major's total refinery throughput of crude oil

C = the integrated major's total crude oil production

ΔP = the change in the price of crude oil

d = the depletion allowance rate

f = the combined rate of state severance taxes and royalties owed the owners of oil lands

$\Delta \pi R$ = the change in the integrated major's after-tax profits from refining

$\Delta \pi C$ = the change in the integrated major's after-tax profits from crude oil production

Suppose the integrated major seeks to shift profits from its refinery operations to its crude operations by raising crude's price. Adoption of this profit-shifting strategy would leave refinery revenues unchanged, but refinery costs would rise by $(\Delta P \cdot R)$ before taxes. Thus, the change in the integrated major's after-tax refining profits would be

$$\Delta \pi R = - (P \cdot R)t$$

Adoption of this profit-shifting strategy raises pretax crude oil revenues by $(\Delta P \cdot C)$. It also yields a tax reduction because of a rise in the depletion allowance of $d(\Delta P \cdot C)$. Partially offsetting the foregoing are higher severance taxes and royalties totaling $f(\Delta P \cdot C)$. Thus, the net change in the integrated major's after-tax crude production profits is

$$\Delta \pi C = (1-f+d) \, (\Delta P \cdot C)t$$

Hence the net profit from adopting this profit-shifting pricing strategy is

$$\Delta\pi R + \Delta\pi C = \Delta P \cdot t \, [(1-f+d) \, C - R]$$

and thus it would be profitable only if

$$[(1-f+d) \, C - R] > 0$$

If the depletion allowance is 22 percent of the gross wellheaded price and the sum of royalties and severance taxes is 15 percent of this price, this inequality will be satisfied only if $C/R > 0.93$.

An analagous derivation appears in M. DeChazeau and A. Kahn, *Integration and Competition in the Petroleum Industry* (New Haven, Conn.: Yale University Press, 1959), pp. 221–222. The DeChazeau-Kahn formulation is less general because it ignores severance taxes and royalties.

[33]Assuming that the marginal tax rate on corporate profits is 48 percent, Marathon's after-tax loss because $1 of profits is shifted from refining to crude production is

$$0.52 \, [\$1.07 \, (0.881) - \$1] = -\$0.0298$$

Standard Oil of Ohio's after-tax loss because $1 of profits are shifted is

$$0.52 \, [\$1.07 \, (0.067) - \$1] = -\$0.483$$

[34]Edward Mitchell, op. cit.; James C. Tanner, "Breakup Could Bring a Gasoline Price Rise and Less Competition," *Wall Street Journal*, February 12, 1976, p. 1, cites recent testimony by Professor Edward Erickson before the Senate Antitrust Subcommittee to the effect that divestiture would raise oil production costs by at least $500 million per year.

[35]A recent survey of academic economists who specialize in the study of industrial organization with special emphasis on the oil industry shows that they give little credence to the oil-company-monopoly charge. In the spring of 1976, 21 of these academic economists answered a questionnaire prepared by Barbara Hobbie (research assistant for this background paper) as part of a master's thesis in Communications Research at the University of Missouri School of Journalism. Of the 21 economists, at least 14 have testified about the oil industry before congressional subcommittees. Nine of the 14 are known to have testified in opposition to oil industry positions on earlier antitrust or privilege issues such as import quotas, the oil depletion allowance, market-demand prorationing, and natural gas pricing.

Fifteen of the economists questioned in this survey (72 percent) either disagreed or strongly disagreed with the statement that "the major, integrated U.S. oil companies currently possess monopoly power in one or more stages of the oil business." Only two (10 percent) opposed this view. In response to a similar question about each of the major stages of the oil business, these experts stated that the greatest concentration of monopoly power exists in pipeline operations. Even so, only 19 percent thought pipelines were monopolized, whereas 43 percent did not. In contrast, tanker operations were judged to be the most competitive stage: 90 percent considered this part of the oil business to be competitive; 5 percent (or one respondent) did not. An average of 75 percent of the economists disagreed or strongly disagreed with statements that the other stages of the oil business—crude oil production, refining, and marketing—are monopolized or that there is a monopoly problem in the production and sale of either coal or natural gas. Twelve percent of the respondents perceived anticompetitive behavior in these areas.

In response to questions about the merits of oil company divestiture, 76 percent of the respondents did not believe it to be a good or effective measure, whereas only 10 percent favored or strongly favored such legislation. The economists largely agreed that divestiture would have little positive effect but potentially high costs. Only one economist thought it would lower prices, whereas 75 percent did not. None of those questioned agreed or strongly agreed that divestiture would cause services to improve. More than half (55 percent) thought such legislation would reduce companies' efficiency; 15 percent saw little relationship between breakup and subsequent inefficiencies. An overwhelming number, 95 percent, agreed (or partially or strongly agreed) that "the oil divestiture issue is sidetracking the U.S. from real energy problem solving." Only one economist partially disagreed with this statement, indicating only a mild preference for divestiture as a means of attacking overall United States energy problems.

[36] *New York Times*, June 9, 1974, and October 13, 1974
[37] Bureau of National Affairs, *Energy Users Report*, December 25, 1975, p. AA-3.
[38] M. A. Adelman, "Is the Oil Shortage Real?" *Foreign Policy*, Winter 1972–73, pp. 101–107.
[39] For a recent elaboration of this plan, see M. A. Adelman, "Oil Import Quota Auctions," *Challenge*, vol. 18, no. 6, January–February 1976, pp. 17–22.
[40] A differential tariff was suggested by the Cabinet Task Force on Oil Import Controls. See U.S. Cabinet Task Force on Oil Import Controls, *The Oil Import Question* (Washington, D.C.: U.S. Government Printing Office, 1970), pp. 134–135.

Chapter 4

[1] Colin Norman, "E.R.D.A. on Energy: A Plan without a Policy," *Technology Review*, vol. 78, no. 3, January 1976, pp. 6 and 66.
[2] Bureau of National Affairs, op. cit., pp. 51-1 and 051 (excerpts from the Environmental Protection Agency's Statement of Program Activities).
[3] Karen Elliot House, "Energy Agency Spends Much Energy to Insure a Long Life, Foes Say," *Wall Street Journal*, February 9, 1976, p. 1
[4] Ibid.
[5] Ibid.

3